Bus Handbook

July 1996

British Bus Publishing

The South Wales Bus Handbook

The South Wales Bus Handbook is part of the Bus Handbook series that details the fleets of selected bus and coach operators. These handbooks are published by *British Bus Publishing* and cover Scotland, Wales and England north of London. The current list is shown at the end of the book. Together with similar books for southern England, published by Capital Transport which we also supply, they provide comprehensive coverage of all the principal operators' fleets in the British Isles. Handbooks for the FirstBus Group and Stagecoach are also published annually.

The operators included in this edition are those who are based, and provide stage and express services in south Wales comprising the former counties of Mid, South and West Glamorgan and Gwent. Also included are a number of operators who provide significant coaching activities.

Quality photographs for inclusion in the series are welcome and a fee is payable. The publishers unfortunately cannot accept responsibility for any loss and request you show your name on each picture or slide. Details of changes to fleet information are also welcome.

To keep the fleet information up to date we recommend the Ian Allan publication, Buses published monthly, or for more detailed information, the PSV Circle monthly news sheets.

The writer and publisher would be glad to hear from readers should any information be available which corrects or enhances that given in this publication.

Series Editor: Bill Potter
Principal Editors for *The South Wales Bus Handbook*:
David Donati & John Jones

Acknowledgements:
We are grateful to Andy Chown, Robert Edworthy, Byron Gage, Ian Kirby, Simon Nicholas, David Thomas, the PSV Circle and the operating companies for their assistance in the compilation of this book.

The cover photograph is by John Jones

Contents correct to July 1996

ISBN 1 897990 18 9
Published by *British Bus Publishing Ltd*
The Vyne, 16 St Margarets Drive, Wellington,
Telford, Shropshire, TF1 3PH
© British Bus Publishing, July 1996

CONTENTS

ARTHUR THOMAS

AA, JT, BE & GA Thomas, Brynteg Garage, 91 Pontardulais Road,
Gorseinon, Swansea, SA4 4FQ

NSX960T	Seddon Pennine 7	Plaxton Supreme IV Express	C49F	1979	Ex Enterprise & SilverDawn, 1996
DWA707V	Ford R1114	Plaxton Supreme IV	C53F	1979	Ex Phillips, Hereford, 1994
NFE313V	Ford R1114	Duple Dominant II Express	C53F	1980	Ex Pullman, Penclawdd, 1992
KVC384V	Ford R1114	Plaxton Supreme IV Express	C53F	1980	Ex Rainbow, Westbury, 1993
KAD353V	Leyland Leopard PSU5C/4R	Plaxton Supreme IV	C57F	1980	Ex Cyril Evans, Senghenydd, 1994
TND110X	Ford R1114	Duple Dominant IV	C53F	1982	Ex Smiths Shearings, 1987

Livery: Cream, red and blue

The mainstay of the Arthur Thomas fleet has for many years been the Ford R1114, though they are gradually being phased out as the marque declines generally. KVC384V is still a regular performer on stage services and is seen leaving Swansea along Kingsway.
John Jones

Arthur Thomas' NFE313V is often used on one of the services out of Swansea by virtue of the "Express" door on its Duple Dominant bodywork. It is seen in March 1996 while loading at the Kingsway, Swansea.
John Jones

BEBB

Bebb Travel plc, The Coach Station, Llantwit Fardre,
Rhondda Cynon Taff, CF38 2HB

M23JDW	Volvo B10M-62	Plaxton Premiére 350	C49FT	1994
M24JDW	Volvo B10M-62	Plaxton Premiére 350	C49FT	1994
M26HNY	Volvo B12T-61	Jonckheere Deauville 65	C49FT	1994
M27HNY	Volvo B12T-61	Jonckheere Deauville 65	C49FT	1994
M28HNY	Volvo B12T-61	Jonckheere Deauville 65	C49FT	1994
M29HNY	Volvo B12T-61	Jonckheere Deauville 65	C49FT	1994
M31KAX	Mercedes-Benz 711D	Autobus Classique 2	C25F	1994
M32KAX	Volvo B10M-62	Plaxton Premiére 350	C49FT	1995
M34KAX	Volvo B10M-62	Plaxton Premiére 350	C49FT	1995
M35KAX	Volvo B10M-62	Plaxton Premiére 350	C49FT	1995
M36KAX	Volvo B10M-62	Plaxton Premiére 350	C49FT	1995
M37KAX	Volvo B10M-62	Plaxton Premiére 350	C49FT	1995
M38KAX	Volvo B10M-62	Plaxton Expressliner 2	C46FT	1995
M39KAX	Volvo B10M-62	Plaxton Expressliner 2	C46FT	1995
M41KAX	Volvo B10M-62	Plaxton Expressliner 2	C46FT	1995
M42KAX	Volvo B10M-62	Plaxton Expressliner 2	C46FT	1995
M43KAX	Volvo B10M-62	Plaxton Expressliner 2	C46FT	1995
M45KAX	Volvo B10M-62	Plaxton Expressliner 2	C46FT	1995
N46MDW	Volvo B10M-62	Plaxton Expressliner 2	C46FT	1995
N47MDW	Volvo B10M-62	Plaxton Expressliner 2	C46FT	1995
N48MDW	Volvo B10M-62	Plaxton Expressliner 2	C46FT	1995
N49MDW	Volvo B10M-62	Plaxton Expressliner 2	C46FT	1995

Bebbs operate the only Welsh examples of the Volvo B12T, four were acquired in 1994 and carry Jonckheere Deauville Monarch bodywork. One of these striking machines M26HNY, is seen in Edward VII Avenue, Cardiff. All are due to be replaced during 1996 by new Volvos of the same type.
John Jones

Although the majority of Bebbs coaches used on National Express contracts are Plaxton Expressliner 2s for Rapide work, several Premiere 350s are also liveried for National Express work. M24JDW is seen at Newport in May 1996 working one of its regular runs out of Cardiff. *John Jones*

Half a dozen of Bebbs all-Volvo B10M coach fleet are Plaxton Premiere 320s in fleet livery and used primarily on contract work and on the Cardiff Express 400 service linking Beddau with the capital. However, N54MDW is seen whilst engaged on private hire work connected with the Five Nations rugby union championship. *John Jones*

Eight Autobus Classique Nouvelle bodied Mercedes-Benz 811Ds entered the Bebb fleet early in 1996, taking over local service work previously performed by Volvo B6s. One of these relatively unusual acquisitions for stage carriage work, N68MDW, is seen leaving Pontypridd bus station in March of this year. *John Jones*

N51MDW	Volvo B10M-62	Plaxton Expressliner 2	C46FT	1995
N52MDW	Volvo B10M-62	Plaxton Expressliner 2	C46FT	1995
N53MDW	Volvo B10M-62	Plaxton Expressliner 2	C46FT	1995
N54MDW	Volvo B10M-62	Plaxton Premiére 320	C57F	1996
N56MDW	Volvo B10M-62	Plaxton Premiére 320	C57F	1996
N57MDW	Volvo B10M-62	Plaxton Premiére 320	C53F	1996
N58MDW	Volvo B10M-62	Plaxton Premiére 320	C53F	1996
N59MDW	Volvo B10M-62	Plaxton Premiére 320	C53F	1996
N61MDW	Volvo B10M-62	Plaxton Premiére 320	C53F	1996
N62MDW	Mercedes-Benz 811D	Autobus Classique Nouvelle	DP33F	1996
N63MDW	Mercedes-Benz 811D	Autobus Classique Nouvelle	DP33F	1996
N64MDW	Mercedes-Benz 811D	Autobus Classique Nouvelle	DP33F	1996
N65MDW	Mercedes-Benz 811D	Autobus Classique Nouvelle	DP33F	1996
N67MDW	Mercedes-Benz 811D	Autobus Classique Nouvelle	DP33F	1996
N68MDW	Mercedes-Benz 811D	Autobus Classique Nouvelle	DP33F	1996
N69MDW	Mercedes-Benz 811D	Autobus Classique Nouvelle	DP33F	1996
N71MDW	Mercedes-Benz 811D	Autobus Classique Nouvelle	DP33F	1996
N91SKG	Volvo B10M-62	Jonckheere Deauville 45	C49FT	1996
N92SKG	Volvo B10M-62	Jonckheere Deauville 45	C49FT	1996
N93SKG	Volvo B10M-62	Jonckheere Deauville 45	C49FT	1996
N94SKG	Volvo B10M-62	Jonckheere Deauville 45	C49FT	1996
N95SKG	Volvo B10M-62	Jonckheere Deauville 45	C49FT	1996
P	Volvo B12T-61	Jonckheere Deauville 65	C49FT	On order
P	Volvo B12T-61	Jonckheere Deauville 65	C49FT	On order
P	Volvo B12T-61	Jonckheere Deauville 65	C49FT	On order
P	Volvo B12T-61	Jonckheere Deauville 65	C49FT	On order
P	Volvo B10M-62	Plaxton Premiére 350	C53F	On order
P	Volvo B10M-62	Plaxton Premiére 350	C53F	On order

Livery: White, blue and orange; National Express 23/4, 32/4-7, 52/3; Rapide 39, 41-3/5-9, 51; AirLink 38.

BREWERS

A E & F R Brewer Ltd, Acacia Avenue, Sandfields Estate,
Port Talbot, Neath & Port Talbot   SA12 7DW

Part of FirstBus plc
Depots: Bridgend Industrial Estate, Bridgend; Tumulus Way, Llandow Trading Estate, Llandow; Heol Ty Gwyn Industrial Estate, Tyle Teg, Maesteg; Acacia Avenue, Sandfields Estate, Port Talbot;

117	C974GCV	Leyland Tiger TRCTL11/3RH	Duple 340	C48FT	1986	Ex Western National, 1995
119	C975GCV	Leyland Tiger TRCTL11/3RH	Duple 340	C48FT	1986	Ex Western National, 1995
122	C976GCV	Leyland Tiger TRCTL11/3RH	Duple 340	C48FT	1986	Ex Western National, 1995
123	C977GCV	Leyland Tiger TRCTL11/3RH	Duple 340	C48FT	1986	Ex Western National, 1995
127	MKH59A	Leyland Tiger TRCTL11/3RH	Duple Caribbean 2	C46FT	1984	Ex SWT, 1992
128	MKH69A	Leyland Tiger TRCTL11/3RH	Duple Caribbean 2	C46FT	1985	Ex SWT, 1993
129	MKH87A	Leyland Tiger TRCTL11/3RH	Duple Caribbean 2	C46FT	1985	Ex SWT, 1993
130	MKH98A	Leyland Tiger TRCTL11/3RH	Duple Caribbean 2	C46FT	1985	Ex SWT, 1994
138	300CUH	Hestair Duple SDA1512	Duple 425	C53FT	1988	Ex Western National, 1993
140	LIL5068	Hestair Duple SDA1512	Duple 425	C50FT	1988	Ex Western National, 1994
144	JWE244W	Leyland Leopard PSU5D/4R	Plaxton Supreme IV	C49FT	1980	Ex Western National, 1995
149	JWE249W	Leyland Leopard PSU5D/4R	Plaxton Supreme IV	C50F	1980	Ex United Welsh Coaches, 1992
151	JWE251W	Leyland Leopard PSU5D/4R	Plaxton Supreme IV	C50F	1980	Ex United Welsh Coaches, 1992
162	EWW945Y	Leyland Tiger TRCTL11/3R	Plaxton Paramount 3200 E	C53F	1983	Ex Rider Group, 1996
163	EWR654Y	Leyland Tiger TRBTL11/2R	Duple Dominant	DP47F	1983	Ex Rider Group, 1996
164	A658KUM	Leyland Tiger TRBTL11/2R	Duple Dominant	DP47F	1983	Ex Rider Group, 1996
165	A670KUM	Leyland Tiger TRBTL11/2R	Duple Dominant	DP47F	1983	Ex Rider Group, 1996
166	B221WEU	Leyland Tiger TRCTL11/3RH	Duple Laser 2	C47FT	1985	Ex Badgerline, 1994
167	VCL461	Leyland Tiger TRCTL11/3RH	Duple Laser 2	C47FT	1984	Ex Badgerline, 1994
170	K9BMS	Dennis Javelin 12SDA2117	Plaxton Premiére 320	C48FT	1993	
171	K13BMS	Dennis Javelin 12SDA2117	Plaxton Premiére 320	C48FT	1993	
172	L6BMS	Dennis Javelin 12SDA2125	Plaxton Premiére 320	C51FT	1994	
173	L8BMS	Dennis Javelin 12SDA2131	Plaxton Premiére 320	C51FT	1994	
174	L14BMS	Dennis Javelin 12SDA2131	Plaxton Premiére 350	C51FT	1994	

Opposite top: **A contender for the most unusual vehicle in this book is Brewers 506, G841PNW. This Van Hool A600 integral is unique in Britain and was acquired in 1994, since which time it has regularly been employed on Brewers longer services. It is seen in Swansea with the city's ruined castle in the background.** *John Jones*

Opposite bottom: **Following the successful operation of eight Plaxton Pointer bodied Dennis Darts in 1994, ten similar vehicles, but with more comfortable seating were received last year. This second batch is widely used on longer distance services and 614, N614MHB, is seen leaving Swansea's Quadrant bus station on a journey of around forty miles to the Welsh capital.** *John Jones*

Brewers 167, VCL461, is one of a pair of Duple Laser 2 bodied Leyland Tigers of 1984-85 vintage acquired from Badgerline in 1994, and retaining their toilets despite receiving bus livery. As if to justify the situation, it is seen while engaged on private hire duties at Taffs Well in April 1996. *John Jones*

The ruins of Swansea Castle again provide the backdrop for a Brewers vehicle as 186, A695OHJ, is seen arriving in the city centre in March 1996. Some of the express work previously carried out by these Alexander TE-bodied Leyland Tigers has now been usurped by the Dennis Darts. *John Jones*

176	RJI8029	Leyland Tiger TRCTL11/3RZ	Plaxton Paramount 3500 II	C49FT	1985	Ex United Welsh Coaches, 1992
177	RJI8030	Leyland Tiger TRCTL11/3RZ	Plaxton Paramount 3500 II	C49FT	1985	Ex United Welsh Coaches, 1992
178	RJI8031	Leyland Tiger TRCTL11/3RZ	Plaxton Paramount 3500 II	C49FT	1985	Ex United Welsh Coaches, 1992
179	B905DHB	Leyland Tiger TRCTL11/3R	Duple Caribbean 2	C51FT	1985	Ex Cardiff Bus, 1995
180	B906DHB	Leyland Tiger TRCTL11/3R	Duple Caribbean 2	C51FT	1985	Ex Cardiff Bus, 1995
181	HHJ374Y	Leyland Tiger TRCTL11/2R	Alexander TE	C53F	1983	Ex Thamesway, 1991
182	HHJ377Y	Leyland Tiger TRCTL11/2R	Alexander TE	C49F	1983	Ex SWT, 1993
183	HHJ379Y	Leyland Tiger TRCTL11/2R	Alexander TE	C53F	1983	Ex Thamesway, 1991
184	A691OHJ	Leyland Tiger TRCTL11/2R	Alexander TE	C53F	1983	Ex Thamesway, 1991
185	A693OHJ	Leyland Tiger TRCTL11/2R	Alexander TE	C49F	1983	Ex SWT, 1993
186	A695OHJ	Leyland Tiger TRCTL11/2R	Alexander TE	C49F	1983	Ex SWT, 1993
188	278TNY	DAF MB230LT615	Plaxton Paramount 3500 III	C53FT	1989	Ex United Welsh Coaches, 1992
189	LIL5069	DAF MB200DKFL600	Plaxton Paramount 3500 II	C51FT	1986	Ex Western National, 1995
190	LIL5070	DAF MB230DKFL615	Duple 340	C48FT	1987	Ex Western National, 1995
191	LIL5071	DAF MB230DKFL615	Duple 340	C53FT	1987	Ex Western National, 1995
192	948RJO	DAF MB230LB615	Plaxton Paramount 3500 III	C51FT	1989	Ex United Welsh Coaches, 1992

201-214

		Mercedes-Benz L608D	Robin Hood	B20F	1985-86 Ex SWT 1992-93

201	C201HTH	204	C204HTH	207	C207HTH	210	C210HTH	213	C213HTH
202	C202HTH	205	C205HTH	208	C208HTH	211	C211HTH	214	C214HTH
203	C203HTH	206	C206HTH	209	C209HTH	212	C212HTH		

217	D217LCY	Mercedes-Benz L608D	Robin Hood	DP19F	1986	Ex SWT 1993
218	WCY701	Mercedes-Benz L608D	Robin Hood	DP19F	1986	Ex SWT 1993
219	D219LCY	Mercedes-Benz L608D	Robin Hood	DP19F	1986	Ex SWT 1993
220	C209HJN	Mercedes-Benz L608D	Reeve Burgess	B20F	1985	Ex Eastern National, 1995
221	C221HJN	Mercedes-Benz L608D	Reeve Burgess	B20F	1985	Ex Eastern National, 1995
222	C478BHY	Mercedes-Benz L608D	Reeve Burgess	B20F	1986	Ex Eastern National, 1995
223	C480BHY	Mercedes-Benz L608D	Reeve Burgess	B20F	1986	Ex Eastern National, 1995
224	C481BHY	Mercedes-Benz L608D	Reeve Burgess	DP20F	1986	Ex Eastern National, 1995

The newest Brewer vehicles to carry United Welsh Coaches livery are the five Plaxton Premiere 320 bodied Dennis Javelins dating from 1993-94. All carry Select index marks and 174, L14BMS, is seen in Cardiff during February 1996 still sporting a badger. *John Jones*

One of Brewers' original batch of Dennis Darts, 606, L606FKG, is seen at Victoria Gardens in Neath, a spot beloved of bus photographers over the years. While the vehicles of Cream Line, Tonmawr have long since disappeared, small operators such as Brian Isaac, Merlyns and Silverline still use the facilities. *Steve Powell*

Brewers stock of Mercedes-Benz L608Ds were originally sourced from SWT but, in 1995, five Reeve Burgess converted examples were received from Eastern National and five finished by Dormobile, from City Line at Bristol. One of the latter, freshly repainted in fleet livery is 227, D520FAE. *Steve Powell*

The role of Brewers Leyland Nationals has now diminished to such an extent that there are now only eight examples remaining in service. 806, WWN806T is seen approaching Bridgend town centre with, typically, the destination blind already set for the return journey, in this case, to the head of the Garw Valley. *John Jones*

225-229
Mercedes-Benz L608D — Dormobile — B20F — 1986 — Ex City Line, 1995

225	D514FAE	226	D517FAE	227	D520FAE	228	D526FAE	229	D527FAE

401-410
Mercedes-Benz 811D — Plaxton Beaver — B31F — 1993

401	K401BAX	403	K403BAX	405	K405BAX	407	K407BAX	409	K409BAX
402	K402BAX	404	K404BAX	406	K406BAX	408	K408BAX	410	K410BAX

411-418
Mercedes-Benz 709D — Reeve Burgess Beaver — B25F* — 1988 — Ex SWT, 1994; 411/3/7 are B23F

411	F601AWN	413	F603AWN	415	F605AWN	417	F318AWN	418	F608AWN
412	F602AWN	414	F604AWN	416	F606AWN				

419	F546EJA	Mercedes-Benz 709D	PMT	DP25F	1988	Ex Rider Group, 1996

423-428
Mercedes-Benz 709D — Reeve Burgess Beaver — B25F* — 1988 — Ex SWT, 1994; *423/8 are B23F

423	E283UCY	424	E284UCY	425	E285UCY	426	E286UCY	428	E288VEP

429	J901MAF	Mercedes-Benz 709D	Wadham Stringer Wessex	B21F	1991	Ex Western National, 1996
430	H825ERV	Mercedes-Benz 709D	Wadham Stringer Wessex	B25F	1991	Ex Western National, 1996
451	E203PWY	Mercedes-Benz 811D	Optare StarRider	DP28F	1987	Ex Rider Group, 1996
452	E204PWY	Mercedes-Benz 811D	Optare StarRider	DP28F	1987	Ex Rider Group, 1996
506	G841PNW	Van Hool A600	Van Hool	B52F	1990	Ex Rider Group, 1994
508	J916WVC	Leyland Lynx LX2R11V18245	Leyland Lynx	B47F	1992	Ex Volvo demonstrator, 1992
509	J375WWK	Leyland Lynx LX2R11V18245	Leyland Lynx	B47F	1992	Ex Volvo demonstrator, 1992
510	K10BMS	Leyland Lynx LX2R11C15Z4A	Leyland Lynx	B47F	1992	
511	K11BMS	Leyland Lynx LX2R11C15Z4A	Leyland Lynx	B47F	1992	
512	K12BMS	Leyland Lynx LX2R11C15Z4A	Leyland Lynx	B47F	1992	

601-608
Dennis Dart 9.8SDL3035 — Plaxton Pointer — B40F — 1994

601	L601FKG	603	L603FKG	605	L605FKG	607	L607FKG	608	L608FKG
602	L602FKG	604	L604FKG	606	L606FKG				

609-618
Dennis Dart 9.8SDL3054 — Plaxton Pointer — DP40F — 1995

609	N609MHB	611	N611MHB	613	N613MHB	615	N615MHB	617	N617MHB
610	N610MHB	612	N612MHB	614	N614MHB	616	N616MHB	618	N618MHB

794-812
Leyland National 11351A/1R — B49F* — 1976-79 — Ex SWT, 1989-1994; *803 is DP52F

794	OEP794R	801	TWN801S	806	WWN806T	810	AWN810V	812	AWN812V
795	OEP795R	803	TWN803S	809	WWN809T				

946	XHK234X	Bristol VRT/SL3/6LXB	Eastern Coach Works	H43/31F	1981	Ex United Welsh Coaches, 1992
947	UAR587W	Bristol VRT/SL3/6LXB	Eastern Coach Works	H43/31F	1981	Ex United Welsh Coaches, 1992
948	UAR588W	Bristol VRT/SL3/6LXB	Eastern Coach Works	H43/31F	1981	Ex United Welsh Coaches, 1992
949	UAR598W	Bristol VRT/SL3/6LXB	Eastern Coach Works	H43/31F	1981	Ex United Welsh Coaches, 1992
959	WTH959T	Bristol VRT/SL3/501	Eastern Coach Works	H43/31F	1979	Ex SWT, 1992

971-988
Bristol VRT/SL3/501 — Eastern Coach Works — H43/31F — 1979-80 — Ex SWT, 1992-94

971	BEP971V	974	BEP974V	981	BEP981V	985	BEP985V	988	ECY988V
972	BEP972V	977	BEP977V	982	BEP982V	986	BEP986V		

Previous Registrations:

278TNY	F200EEP	LIL5069	C792MVH	MKH98A	B130CTH
300CUH	E218CFJ	LIL5070	E340WTT	RJI8029	B34UNW, SWN159, 948RJO
948RJO	G500JEP	LIL5071	E978WTA	RJI8030	B35UNW, 300CUH
G841PNW	G680TKE, A6RLR	MKH59A	B127CTH	RJI8031	B36UNW, WCY701
J901MAF	J6EDE	MKH69A	B128CTH	VCL461	B223WEU
LIL5068	E207BOD	MKH87A	B129CTH	WCY701	D218LCY

Liveries: Red, white and yellow (buses); white, red and green (coaches); white and green (Village Bus) 213/4; white and blue (Rail Link) 224; white (National Express) 122

BRIAN ISAAC

Brian Isaac Coaches Ltd, Coach Hire Centre, Kemys Way, Swansea Enterprise Park, Morriston, Swansea, SA6 8QF

26	XCY372T	Bedford YMT	Duple Dominant II Express	C53F	1979	Ex D Coaches, Morriston, 1980
34	AUJ711T	Bedford YMT	Duple Dominant II	C53F	1979	Ex Go-Whittle, Highley, 1981
47	MDV143W	Bedford YMT	Duple Dominant II	C53F	1980	Ex Snell, Newton Abbot, 1984
54	D402OWN	Mercedes-Benz L207D	Reeve Burgess	M12	1987	
55	D403OWN	Bedford CF	Dormobile	M12	1987	
56	D404OWN	Mercedes-Benz L207D	Reeve Burgess	M12	1987	
65	540CCY	Leyland Leopard PSU5A/4R	Duple Dominant I	C51F	1976	Ex Brewers, 1988
74	A310UEP	Mercedes-Benz L307D	Devon Conversions	M12	1984	Ex Collins, Roch, 1989
77	431DWN	Dennis Javelin 12SDA1907	Duple 320	C53FT	1991	
81	D73TLV	Freight Rover Sherpa	Carlyle	B20F	1987	Ex North Western, 1991
82	YSV720	Volvo B58-61	Duple Dominant II	C53F	1979	Ex Taunton Coaches, 1992
83	BWE210T	Leyland Leopard PSU5C/4R	Duple Dominant II	C51F	1979	Ex Hanson, Kenilworth, 1992
84	HJI980	Volvo B10M-61	Plaxton Paramount 3500	C49FT	1984	Ex Forget-me-not, Otley, 1993
86	D132NUS	Mercedes-Benz L608D	Alexander AM	B20F	1986	Ex Caldwell, Greenock, 1993
87	ANJ305T	Leyland Leopard PSU3E/4R	Plaxton Supreme III Express	C49F	1978	Ex Blackburn, 1993
88	ANJ312T	Leyland Leopard PSU3E/4R	Plaxton Supreme III Express	C49F	1979	Ex Blackburn, 1993
89	ANJ314T	Leyland Leopard PSU3E/4R	Plaxton Supreme III Express	C49F	1979	Ex Blackburn, 1993
90	L500BWN	Dennis Javelin 12SDA2117	Plaxton Premiére 320	C51FT	1993	
90	WOI3003	Dennis Javelin 12SDA1907	Duple 320	C53FT	1988	Ex Ipswich, 1993
91	WOI3004	Dennis Javelin 12SDA1907	Duple 320	C53FT	1988	Ex Ipswich, 1993
101	G780HFV	Iveco Daily 45.10	Howells	C21F	1989	Ex Beavis, Bussage, 1994
102	H859NOC	Iveco Daily 49.10	Carlyle Dailybus 2	B25F	1991	Ex RoadRunner, Motherwell, 1994
	KMW179P	Daimler Fleetline CRG6LX	Eastern Coach Works	H43/31F	1975	Ex Waddon, Bedwas, 1995
	CWU142T	Leyland Fleetline FE30AGR	Roe	H43/33F	1978	Ex Rider Group, 1995
	CWU145T	Leyland Fleetline FE30AGR	Roe	H43/33F	1978	Ex Rider Group, 1995
	CWU147T	Leyland Fleetline FE30AGR	Roe	H43/33F	1978	Ex Rider Group, 1995
	KWG433W	Bedford YMT	Plaxton Supreme IV	C53F	1981	Ex Alan Morris, Swansea, 1995
	JWE245W	Leyland Leopard PSU5D/4R	Plaxton Supreme IV	C50F	1981	Ex Brewers, 1996
	JWE247W	Leyland Leopard PSU5D/4R	Plaxton Supreme IV	C50F	1981	Ex Brewers, 1996
	JWE248W	Leyland Leopard PSU5D/4R	Plaxton Supreme IV	C50F	1981	Ex Brewers, 1996
	JWE250W	Leyland Leopard PSU5D/4R	Plaxton Supreme IV	C50F	1981	Ex Brewers, 1996
	E253ACC	Iveco Daily 49.10	Robin Hood City Nippy	B21F	1988	Ex Midland Fox, 1996
	F613PWS	Iveco Daily 49.10	Dormobile Routemaker	B20F	1989	Ex City Line, 1996
	N313VWN	Dennis Javelin 12SDA2155	Berkhof Excellence 1000LD	C51FT	1996	

Previous Registrations:

431DWN	H510RCY	WOI3003	E340KBJ
540CCY	URN208R	WOI3004	E341KDX
HJI980	5019BT, A778RUG	YSV720	AFH5T, 5904WF, GDF107T, XFJ379, KYB559T

Livery: White, blue and magenta

An above average number of arrivals joined the Brian Isaac fleet in 1993, including a pair of Duple 320-bodied Dennis Javelins from Ipswich. The second of these, 91, WOI3004, which was registered E341KDX when new, is seen in this view.
Byron Gage

The first double deckers for the Brian Isaac fleet were received in 1995 in the shape of a former Thamesdown Leyland Fleetline with relatively uncommon bodywork from Eastern Coach Works, and a trio of Fleetlines from the Rider Group. One of these, which have attractive Roe bodywork, is CWU142T, looking particularly well turned out in Isaacs livery. *Byron Gage*

Flagship of the Brian Isaac fleet for three years was this Dennis Javelin with Plaxton Premiere 320 body. It is one of four Javelins in the fleet, other coaches being of Bedford, Leyland and Volvo manufacture. L500BWN is allocated fleet number 90 as is ex-Ipswich Javelin WOI3003. *Byron Gage*

Duple Dominant III coachwork as exemplified by Burrows' WGB298W proved briefly popular in the early 1980s. Shallow trapezoid windows had been employed in coaches in the USA for many years and became a feature of those used on Anglo-Scottish express services, particularly those of Eastern Scottish and Western SMT, from the late 1960s. Coincidentally, this coach was acquired from a Scottish operator. *Byron Gage*

The majority of the Burrows coach fleet is DAF powered, the newest example being Duple 340 bodied G300JEP, seen attending the Royal Welsh Show at Llanelwedd near Builth Wells. It was acquired from Brewers when that operator purchased several buses with Burrows Bridgend-Nantymoel service in 1993. *David Donati*

BURROWS

R & D Burrows Ltd, Water Street, Ogmore Vale, Bridgend, CF32 7AN

OTO560M	Leyland Atlantean AN68/1R	East Lancashire	H47/30D	1974	Ex Maidstone & District, 1992
JJG5P	Leyland Atlantean AN68/1R	Eastern Coach Works	H43/31F	1976	Ex Mercury Passenger Services, Hoo, 1995
PPH473R	Bristol VRT/SL3/501	Eastern Coach Works	H43/31F	1977	Ex Brewers, 1993
DUP743S	Bristol VRT/SL3/6LXB	Eastern Coach Works	H43/31F	1978	Ex Reading, 1993
WGB298W	Leyland Leopard PSU5C/4R	Duple Dominant IV	C57F	1981	Ex Irvine, Law, 1993
TIB5912	Bova EL26/581	Bova Europa	C46FT	1983	Ex International Coachways, Dundee, 1993
TIB5909	DAF SB2300DHS585	Berkhof Esprite 350	C49FT	1983	Ex Travelfar, Henfield, 1990
C684WKS	DAF MB230DKVL615	Plaxton Paramount 3500 II	C53F	1986	Ex Austin, Earlston, 1996
F304JFT	Leyland Tiger TRCL10/3ARZM	Plaxton Paramount 3500 III	C49FT	1988	Ex Classic, Annfield Plain, 1996
G300JEP	DAF SB2305DHS585	Duple 340	C51FT	1989	Ex Brewers, 1993

Previous Registrations:

C684WKS	C704LMA, 1810VT, C863NCA, BAZ4773	TIB5912	YGY642Y
TIB5909	A647NOO, 9195PU, A330NJK	WGB298W	XVG684W,123TRL

Livery: Blue and white

Burrows have operated double deckers on school contracts for many years, usually Leyland Atlanteans and often former Bournemouth examples. The two Atlanteans currently operated were sourced elsewhere and OTO560M is still in full Boroline Maidstone livery though acquired from Maidstone & District. *David Donati*

C & E TRAVEL

E Hewitt; C Hewitt, Mount Durand, The Firs, Llanover Road, Blaenavon,
Blaenau Gwent, NP4 9HS

Depot : Gilchrist Thomas Industrial Estate, Blaenavon

YPB840T	Bedford YLQ	Duple Dominant II	C45F	1979	Ex Allways, Halfway, 1991
BCK942V	Bedford YMT	Duple Dominant II	C53F	1980	Ex Gastonia Taxis, Godalming, 1993
RHM928Y	Mercedes-Benz L307D	Devon Conversions	M12	1983	Ex Waddon, Bedwas, 1996
E657VHF	Iveco Daily 40.8	Wright	B24F	1988	Ex Liverpool Social Services, 1996
E962JBC	Freight Rover Sherpa (Ford)	Freight Rover	M16	1988	Ex Leicestershire HA, 1993
E250MHX	Iveco Daily 49.10	Robin Hood City Nippy	B21F	1988	Ex Vale of Manchester, 1994

Livery: White

CAPITOL COACHES

J D Cleverly Ltd, 2 Somerset Road, Cwmbran, Torfaen, NP44 1QX

NBZ1844	Leyland Tiger TRCTL11/3R	Plaxton Viewmaster IV	C53F	1982	Ex Truman's, Pontypool, 1996
B912AAX	Bedford YNT	Plaxton Paramount 3200	C53F	1984	
B913AAX	Bedford YNT	Plaxton Paramount 3200	C53F	1984	
C101DWR	Volvo B10M-61	Plaxton Paramount 3500 II	C50F	1986	Ex Wallace Arnold, 1991
C111DWR	Volvo B10M-61	Plaxton Paramount 3500 II	C50F	1986	Ex Wallace Arnold, 1991
C113DWR	Volvo B10M-61	Plaxton Paramount 3500 II	C50F	1986	Ex Vale of Llangollen, 1991
C114DWR	Volvo B10M-61	Plaxton Paramount 3500 II	C50F	1986	Ex Vale of Llangollen, 1991
C116DWR	Volvo B10M-61	Plaxton Paramount 3500 II	C50F	1986	Ex Wallace Arnold, 1991
C123DWR	Volvo B10M-61	Plaxton Paramount 3500 II	C50F	1986	Ex Wallace Arnold, 1991
D213LWX	Volvo B10M-61	Duple 340	C50F	1987	Ex Flight's, Birmingham, 1992
D214LWX	Volvo B10M-61	Duple 340	C50F	1987	Ex Wallace Arnold, 1992
D215LWX	Volvo B10M-61	Duple 340	C50F	1987	Ex Classic Tours, Paignton, 1992
D216LWX	Volvo B10M-61	Duple 340	C50F	1987	Ex Flight's, Birmingham, 1992
F22CWO	Leyland Tiger TRCL10/3ARZM	Plaxton Paramount 3500 III	C53FT	1989	
F23CWO	Leyland Tiger TRCL10/3ARZM	Plaxton Paramount 3500 III	C53FT	1989	
F25CWO	Leyland Tiger TRCL10/3ARZM	Plaxton Paramount 3500 III	C53FT	1989	
G117XRE	Volvo B10M-60	Plaxton Expressliner	C51FT	1989	Ex Travellers, Hounslow, 1996
SDZ6287	Volvo B10M-60	Plaxton Expressliner	C51FT	1989	Ex Logan, Dunloy, 1996
G517LWU	Volvo B10M-60	Plaxton Paramount 3500 III	C50F	1990	Ex Silver Coach Lines, 1996
G450DSB	Volvo B10M-60	Duple 340	C55F	1990	Ex West Coast Motors, 1996
H610UWR	Volvo B10M-60	Plaxton Paramount 3500 III	C48FT	1991	Ex Wallace Arnold, 1994
H611UWR	Volvo B10M-60	Plaxton Paramount 3500 III	C48FT	1991	Ex Wallace Arnold, 1994
M848LTX	Toyota Coaster HZB50R	Caetano Optimo III	C21F	1995	
N731PWO	Ford Transit VE6	Ford	M14	1996	
N707MWO	Volvo B10M-62	Plaxton Première 350	C51FT	1995	
N808MWO	Volvo B10M-62	Plaxton Première 350	C51FT	1995	

Livery: White, red and blue; duo blue and white (Morris Bros) B912/3AAX

Previous Registrations:

NBZ1844	UVR1X, 647JOE, RND64X	SDZ6287	G118XRE

The majority of Capitol Coaches fleet are Volvo B10Ms, many of which originated with Wallace Arnold. Oldest of them are 1986 examples acquired when five years old including C123DWR, seen here working a school contract at Monmouth Girls School. *David Donati*

Capitol Coaches operates one of the popular Caetano Optimo bodied Toyota Coasters, providing very comfortable transport for the smaller party. M848LTX is seen when new approaching Barry Island to attend the Welsh Bus and Coach Rally in June 1995. *John Jones*

CARDIFF BLUEBIRD

Cardiff Bluebird Ltd, 307 Penarth Road, Grangetown, Cardiff CF1 7TT

1	M100CBB	Dennis Dart 9.8SDL3040	Plaxton Pointer	B40F	1995	
2	M200CBB	Dennis Dart 9.8SDL3040	Plaxton Pointer	B40F	1995	
8	MAU618P	Leyland Atlantean AN68/1R	East Lancashire	H47/31D	1975	Ex City of Nottingham, 1994
9	MAU619P	Leyland Atlantean AN68/1R	East Lancashire	H47/31D	1976	Ex City of Nottingham, 1994
10	MAU620P	Leyland Atlantean AN68/1R	East Lancashire	H47/31D	1976	Ex City of Nottingham, 1994
11	MAU621P	Leyland Atlantean AN68/1R	East Lancashire	H47/31D	1976	Ex City of Nottingham, 1994
17	E837BTN	MCW MetroRider MF150/27	MCW	B21F	1987	Ex Kentish Bus, 1996
18	D708TWM	Renault-Dodge S56	Northern Counties	B22F	1987	Ex City Buslines, Birmingham, 1995
19	D709TWM	Renault-Dodge S56	Northern Counties	B22F	1987	Ex Clydeside, 1995
21	D861NVS	Renault-Dodge S56	Reeve Burgess	B25F	1986	Ex Luton & District, 1995
22	D862NVS	Renault-Dodge S56	Reeve Burgess	B25F	1986	Ex Luton & District, 1995
24	D864NVS	Renault-Dodge S56	Reeve Burgess	B25F	1986	Ex Luton & District, 1995
25	D865NVS	Renault-Dodge S56	Reeve Burgess	B25F	1986	Ex Luton & District, 1995

Opposite, top: The Cardiff Bluebird double deck fleet consists of Leyland Atlanteans and MCW Metrobuses. Number 78, UWW518X, is one of a pair of Metrobuses acquired from Black Prince, Morley, but new to West Yorkshire PTE, and is seen in Park Place, Cardiff on one of the all too rare sunny days in the spring of 1996. *John Jones*

Opposite, bottom: The only new vehicles to enter service with Cardiff Bluebird to date are a pair of Plaxton Pointer bodied Dennis Darts. Number 2, M200CBB, is seen in Greyfriars Road approaching the city centre on one of several cross-city routes, all of which are operated in competition with Cardiff Bus. *John Jones*

Without reference to the registration plate, the original owner of Cardiff Bluebird 10 will be readily apparent to many enthusiasts. The East Lancashire body on MAU620P and its three fellows is of typical Nottingham design and it is a tribute to their ruggedness that though twenty years old, they still ply the streets of Cardiff on busy routes six days a week. *John Jones*

Cardiff Bluebird took the opportunity to supplement its MCW MetroRider stock in 1995 when six became available following the demise of Darlington Transport. No. 83, E270REP, is one of four new to SWT, all of which, unusually, are fitted with manual transmission. Beatties store in Kingsway, Cardiff provides the backdrop for this view. *John Jones*

31	E631KYW	MCW MetroRider MF150/46	MCW	B25F	1987	Ex Parfitt's, 1995
32	E632KYW	MCW MetroRider MF150/46	MCW	B25F	1987	Ex London Buses, 1993
34	E634KYW	MCW MetroRider MF150/46	MCW	B25F	1987	Ex London Buses, 1993
36	F116EKO	MCW MetroRider MF159/2	MCW	B25F	1988	Ex Kentish Bus, 1996
38	E138KYW	MCW MetroRider MF150/38	MCW	B25F	1987	Ex London Buses, 1993
39	E639KYW	MCW MetroRider MF150/46	MCW	B25F	1987	Ex London Buses, 1993
41	E811UDT	MCW MetroRider MF150/15	MCW	B23F	1987	Ex City Buslines, Birmingham, 1995
42	E812UDT	MCW MetroRider MF150/15	MCW	B23F	1987	Ex Stevensons, 1993
47	D477PON	MCW MetroRider MF150/14	MCW	B23F	1987	Ex Darlington, 1995
49	D469PON	MCW MetroRider MF150/14	MCW	B23F	1987	Ex Darlington, 1995
51	JHE141W	MCW Metrobus DR104/6	MCW	H45/31F	1980	Ex Yellow Bus, Stoke Mandeville, 1995
52	JHE143W	MCW Metrobus DR104/6	MCW	H45/31F	1980	Ex Yellow Bus, Stoke Mandeville, 1995
53	JHE163W	MCW Metrobus DR104/6	MCW	H45/31F	1980	Ex Yellow Bus, Stoke Mandeville, 1995
54	JHE164W	MCW Metrobus DR104/6	MCW	H45/31F	1980	Ex Yellow Bus, Stoke Mandeville, 1995
59	JHE139W	MCW Metrobus DR104/6	MCW	H45/31F	1980	Ex Yellow Bus, Stoke Mandeville, 1995
61	DWJ563V	Leyland Atlantean AN68A/1R	Roe	H45/29D	1979	Ex Camms, Nottingham, 1993
63	XWG652T	Leyland Atlantean AN68A/1R	Roe	H45/29D	1979	Ex Rhodeservice, Yeadon, 1993
64	CWG760V	Leyland Atlantean AN68A/1R	Roe	H45/29D	1979	Ex Camms, Nottingham, 1993
67	ONN574P	Leyland Atlantean AN68/1R	Eastern Coach Works	H43/31F	1976	Ex Trent (Barton), 1994
71	UWW519X	MCW Metrobus DR101/5	Alexander RH	H43/32F	1982	Ex Black Prince, Morley, 1994
72	ULS621X	MCW Metrobus DR102/28	Alexander RL	H45/33F	1982	Ex Capital Citybus, 1995
78	UWW518X	MCW Metrobus DR101/5	Alexander RH	H43/32F	1982	Ex Black Prince, Morley, 1994
80	E261REP	MCW MetroRider MF150/16	MCW	B25F	1987	Ex Darlington, 1995
81	E262REP	MCW MetroRider MF150/16	MCW	B25F	1987	Ex Darlington, 1995
82	E269REP	MCW MetroRider MF150/16	MCW	B25F	1987	Ex Darlington, 1995
83	E270REP	MCW MetroRider MF150/16	MCW	B25F	1987	Ex Darlington, 1995
90	D420NNA	Renault-Dodge S46	Northern Counties	B22F	1987	Ex Midland, 1995
92	D412NNA	Renault-Dodge S46	Northern Counties	B22F	1987	Ex North Western, 1995
130	MHS30P	Leyland Leopard PSU3C/4R	Alexander AYS	B53F	1976	Ex Clydeside 2000, 1995

Livery: Blue and white

CARDIFF BUS

Cardiff City Transport Services Ltd, Sloper Road, Leckwith, Cardiff, CF1 8AF.

023-029		Dennis Dart 9.8SDL3054		Alexander Dash		B41F		1995	
023	N23OBO	025	N25OBO	027	N27OBO	028	N28OBO	029	N29OBO
024	N24OBO	026	N26OBO						

042	E142TBO	MCW MetroRider MF150/78	MCW		B23F		1988

101-109		Optare MetroRider MR15		Optare		B31F		1994-95 *101-4 are DP31F	
101	L101GBO	103	L103GBO	105	L105GBO	107	M107JHB	109	M109JHB
102	L102GBO	104	L104GBO	106	L106GBO	108	M108JHB		

110-133		Optare MetroRider MR15		Optare		B31F		1995	
110	M110KBO	116	M116KBO	121	M121KBO	126	M126KBO	130	M130KBO
112	M112KBO	117	M117KBO	122	M122KBO	127	M127KBO	131	M131KBO
113	M113KBO	118	M118KBO	123	M123KBO	128	M128KBO	132	M132KBO
114	M114KBO	119	M119KBO	124	M124KBO	129	M129KBO	133	M133KBO
115	M115KBO	120	M120KBO	125	M125KBO				

134-143		Optare MetroRider MR15		Optare		B31F		1996	
134	N134PTG	136	N136PTG	138	N138PTG	140	N140PTG	142	N142PTG
135	N135PTG	137	N137PTG	139	N139PTG	141	N141PTG	143	N143PTG

150-155		MCW MetroRider MF150/119		MCW		B23F		1988	
150	F150AWO	152	F152AWO	153	F153AWO	154	F154AWO	155	F155AWO
151	F151AWO								

156-165		MCW MetroRider MF154/19*		MCW		B31F*		1988 *162-5 are DP31F and MF154/20	
156	F156AWO	158	F158AWO	160	F160AWO	162	F162AWO	164	F164AWO
157	F157AWO	159	F159AWO	161	F161AWO	163	F163AWO	165	F165AWO

166-175		Optare MetroRider MR01		Optare		B31F		1990-91	
166	G166HWO	168	H168OTG	170	H170OTG	172	H172RBO	174	H174RBO
167	G167HWO	169	H169OTG	171	H171OTG	173	H173RBO	175	H175RBO

All of Cardiff Bus' Optare MetroRiders, of which there are now seventy-four, are of the long wheelbase, narrow bodied variety. One of the 1992 batch is 183, K183YDW, seen in the grounds of the University Hospital of Wales, on part of the circuitous route taken by route 36 from Gabalfa to the Central bus station. *John Jones*

When production of the Leyland Lynx ended, Cardiff Bus turned to Scania for its next two batches of saloons and in all, twenty one N113CRBs were received. The last seven were fitted with Alexander Strider bodywork similar to those at neighbouring Newport except for a slightly increased seating capacity. Seen in Wood Street approaching the bus station is 288, L288ETG. *John Jones*

176-187

				Optare MetroRider MR01		Optare			B31F		1992		
176	J176WAX	179	J179WAX	182	J182WAX	184	K184YDW	186	K186YDW
177	J177WAX	180	J180WAX	183	K183YDW	185	K185YDW	187	K187YDW
178	J178WAX	181	J181WAX						

188-197

Optare MetroRider MR15   Optare   B31F   1994

188	L188DDW	190	L190DDW	192	L192DDW	194	L194DDW	196	L196DDW
189	L189DDW	191	L191DDW	193	L193DDW	195	L195DDW	197	L197DDW

231-240

Leyland Lynx LX112L10ZR1R   Leyland   B51F*   1989   *237-240 are DP47F

231	F231CNY	233	F233CNY	235	F235CNY	237	F237CNY	239	F239CNY
232	F232CNY	234	F234CNY	236	F236CNY	238	F238CNY	240	F240CNY

241-259

Leyland Lynx LX2R11C15Z4R   Leyland   B49F   1989-90

241	F241CNY	245	F245CNY	249	G249HUH	253	G253HUH	257	G257HUH
242	F242CNY	246	F246CNY	250	G250HUH	254	G254HUH	258	G258HUH
243	F243CNY	247	F247CNY	251	G251HUH	255	G255HUH	259	G259HUH
244	F244CNY	248	F248CNY	252	G252HUH	256	G256HUH		

260-271

Leyland Lynx LX2R11C15Z4S   Leyland Lynx 2   B49F   1991   260 Ex VL Bus, 1991

260	H49NDU	263	J263UDW	266	J266UDW	268	J268UDW	270	J270UDW
261	J261UDW	264	J264UDW	267	J267UDW	269	J269UDW	271	J271UDW
262	J262UDW	265	J265UDW						

Opposite, top: **Cardiff Bus has been an enthusiastic operator of Alexander bodied buses since 1966 when thirty-seven Guy Arab Vs were received. The latest products are very different, being mounted on Dennis Dart chassis and representing, other than the Rees & Williams example now with SWT, the only Alexander Dash-bodied models with a Welsh operator. Number 024, N24OBO, is seen in Park Place in April 1996.** *John Jones*

Opposite, bottom: **Many of Cardiff Buses earlier MCW MetroRiders have been replaced by new MetroRiders built by Optare, with over fifty delivered since 1994. The latest batch, comprising ten vehicles, culminates with 143, N143PTG, seen in Wood Street, Cardiff in May of this year.** *John Jones*

272-286 — Scania N113CRB — Plaxton Verde — B51F — 1992

272	J272UWO	275	J275UWO	278	J278UWO	282	J282UWO	285	J285UWO
273	J273UWO	276	J276UWO	279	J279UWO	283	J283UWO	286	J286UWO
274	J274UWO	277	J277UWO	281	J281UWO	284	J284UWO		

287-293 — Scania N113CRB — Alexander Strider — B50F — 1994

287	L287ETG	289	L289ETG	291	L291ETG	292	L292ETG	293	L293ETG
288	L288ETG	290	L290ETG						

335-396 — Bristol VRT/SL3/6LXB — Alexander AL — H44/31F* — 1978-80 *359/60 are CO44/31F

335	WTG335T	346	WTG346T	356	WTG356T	370	WTG370T	384	CTX384V
336	WTG336T	347	WTG347T	359	WTG359T	373	WTG373T	386	CTX386V
338	WTG338T	348	WTG348T	360	WTG360T	374	WTG374T	388	CTX388V
339	WTG339T	349	WTG349T	361	WTG361T	375	WTG375T	391	CTX391V
340	WTG340T	350	WTG350T	362	WTG362T	376	WTG376T	392	CTX392V
341	WTG341T	351	WTG351T	365	WTG365T	377	WTG377T	393	CTX393V
342	WTG342T	353	WTG353T	367	WTG367T	380	WTG380T	394	CTX394V
344	WTG344T	354	WTG354T	368	WTG368T	381	WTG381T	395	CTX395V
345	WTG345T	355	WTG355T	369	WTG369T	382	CTX382V	396	CTX396V

401-436 — Volvo-Ailsa B55-10 MkIII — Northern Counties — H39/35F — 1982-84

401	NDW401X	409	NDW409X	416	NDW416X	423	RKG423Y	430	A430VNY
402	NDW402X	410	NDW410X	417	NDW417X	424	RKG424Y	431	A431VNY
403	NDW403X	411	NDW411X	418	NDW418X	425	RKG425Y	432	A432VNY
404	NDW404X	412	NDW412X	419	RKG419Y	426	RKG426Y	433	A433VNY
405	NDW405X	413	NDW413X	420	RKG420Y	427	RKG427Y	434	A434VNY
406	NDW406X	414	NDW414X	421	RKG421Y	428	A428VNY	435	A435VNY
407	NDW407X	415	NDW415X	422	RKG422Y	429	A429VNY	436	A436VNY
408	NDW408X								

437-446 — Volvo-Ailsa B55-10 MkIII — Alexander RV — H45/37F — 1984 — Ex MTL (Merseybus), 1996

437	A151HLV	439	A154HLV	441	A158HLV	443	A160HLV	445	A162HLV
438	A152HLV	440	A156HLV	442	A159HLV	444	A161HLV	446	A163HLV

447	DEM821Y	Volvo-Ailsa B55-10 MkIII	Alexander RV	H45/31F	1982	Ex MTL (Merseybus), 1996
448	DEM822Y	Volvo-Ailsa B55-10 MkIII	Alexander RV	H45/31F	1982	Ex MTL (Merseybus), 1996

501-519 — Leyland Olympian ONLXB/1R — East Lancashire — H43/31F — 1981-84 510 is H43/29F

501	LBO501X	505	RBO505Y	509	RBO509Y	513	A513VKG	517	A517VKG
502	RBO502Y	506	RBO506Y	510	RBO510Y	514	A514VKG	518	A518VKG
503	RBO503Y	507	RBO507Y	511	A511VKG	515	A515VKG	519	A519VKG
504	RBO504Y	508	RBO508Y	512	A512VKG	516	A516VKG		

551-567 — Leyland Olympian ONLXB/1R — East Lancashire — H43/31F — 1984-85 560-7 are H43/27F

551	B551ATX	555	B555ATX	559	B559ATX	562	C562GWO	565	C565GWO
552	B552ATX	556	B556ATX	560	C560GWO	563	C563GWO	566	C566GWO
553	B553ATX	557	B557ATX	561	C561GWO	564	C564GWO	567	C567GWO
554	B554ATX	558	B558ATX						

601-607 — Scania N113DRB — Alexander RH — H47/33F — 1990

601	G601KTX	603	G603KTX	605	G605KTX	606	G606KTX	607	G607KTX
602	G602KTX	604	G604KTX						

608	J608VDW	Scania N113DRB	Alexander RH	H47/31F	1992	
609	J609VDW	Scania N113DRB	Alexander RH	H47/31F	1992	
610	J610VDW	Scania N113DRB	Alexander RH	H47/31F	1992	

Liveries: Orange and white (double decks); orange, white and brown (single decks)

The thirty six Volvo-Ailsas received by Cardiff Bus in 1982-84 were relatively unusual in carrying Northern Counties bodywork, the other principal operator of similar buses being Derby. They all continue to give excellent service and are presently being supplemented by twelve Alexander bodied examples from Merseybus which will allow further withdrawals of Bristol VRTs. 402 (NDW402X) is seen using the Park Place bus lane in April 1996. *John Jones*

The longest route operated by Cardiff Bus is that shared with Islwyn Transport to Tredegar, a distance of some thirty three miles. Cardiff Bus journeys, except for evenings and Sundays when MetroRiders are used, are performed by Leyland Olympians of the 551-567 series. These have a high-ratio rear axle and were once fitted with high-backed seats. They are not as high as Cardiffs other 'deckers and will pass with ease under the low railway bridge at Aber near Caerphilly. No 558 (B558ATX) stirs up the leaves at Blackwood last autumn. *John Jones*

27

CASTELL COACHES

B R Kerslake, Units 3 & 4, European Terminal Building, Pant Glas Ind Est, Trethomas, Caerphilly, NP1 8AR

SUH859M	Leyland Leopard PSU3B/4R	Plaxton Elite III	C53F	1974	Ex Phil Henderson, Pen-y-graig, 1994
AUJ722T	Bedford YLQ	Duple Dominant II	C45F	1979	Ex Victoria Motorways, Treorchy, 1989
OPR511W	Ford R1114	Plaxton Supreme IV	C49F	1981	Ex Phil Henderson, Pen-y-graig, 1991
D30VEY	DAF MB200DKFL600	Duple 340	C57F	1987	Ex Clark & Goodman, Pailton, 1991
F233SMC	Peugeot-Talbot Express	Adams	M16	1988	
F594BTG	Leyland Tiger TRCL10/3ARZM	Plaxton Paramount 3500 III	C49FT	1989	Ex Waddon, Bedwas, 1992
F127AEL	Volvo B10M-60	Plaxton Paramount 3200 III	C53F	1989	Ex Excelsior, Bournemouth, 1995
F128AEL	Volvo B10M-60	Plaxton Paramount 3200 III	C53F	1989	Ex Excelsior, Bournemouth, 1995
G545RVJ	Mercedes-Benz 508D	Premier	C19F	1989	Ex van, 1995
H607UWR	Volvo B10M-60	Plaxton Paramount 3500 III	C48FT	1991	Ex Wallace Arnold, 1994
H904AHS	Volvo B10M-60	Plaxton Paramount 3500 III	C53F	1991	Ex Plymouth Citybus, 1994
J344MBX	Renault Master T35D	Cymric	M16	1991	
J23VWO	Volvo B10M-60	Plaxton Paramount 3500 III	C51FT	1992	Ex Bebb, Llantwit Fardre, 1994
L354MKU	Mercedes-Benz 814D	Plaxton Beaver	C33F	1993	
L559YYS	Volvo B10M-60	Van Hool Alizée	C53F	1993	Ex Clarkes of London, 1995
L141AHS	Volvo B10M-60	Van Hool Alizée	C53F	1993	Ex Park's, 1995
N103BHL	Mercedes-Benz 814D	Plaxton Beaver	C33F	1995	

Previous Registrations:

F127AEL	F445WEX, A13EXC	L141AHS	LSK473, KSK948
F128AEL	F446WEX, A16EXC	L559YYS	LSK870, KSK951

Livery: White, orange, red and yellow

COASTAL CONTINENTAL

Coastal Continental Coachline Ltd, Hinds Garage, 15 Dock View Road, Barry, Vale of Glamorgan CF63 4JP

ROK452M	Daimler Fleetline CRG6LX	East Lancashire	H44/30F	1974	Ex West Midlands Travel, 1988
ROK459M	Daimler Fleetline CRG6LX	East Lancashire	H44/30F	1974	Ex Blackhorse Coaches, 1989
LHT729P	Bristol VRT/SL3/6LXB	Eastern Coach Works	H43/27D	1976	Ex City Line, 1990
OKG292R	Ford R1114	Plaxton Supreme III	C53F	1976	
OCU420R	Leyland Leopard PSU3C/4R	Plaxton Supreme III	C51F	1977	Ex Hunter, Seaton Delaval, 1981
DFB680W	Leyland Leopard PSU3E/4R	Duple Dominant II Express	C53F	1977	Ex Thomas of Barry, 1989
CUP759W	Bedford VAS5	Duple Dominant	C29F	1980	Ex Parkin, Saham Toney, 1993

Castell Coaches is a varied fleet but the majority of the coaches are based on Volvo B10M chassis and, apart from a pair of Van Hool Alizee examples, all have Plaxton Paramount bodywork. J73VWO is one of three, a 1992 example purchased after two years from Bebb, Wales most prolific Volvo coach operator. *John Jones*

Coastal DBF680W is a Duple Dominant bodied Leyland Leopard pictured at its normal weekday parking spot in Cardiff. It has been based in Barry all its life, having been new to Thomas Motors, one of the oldest established South Wales operators, which has recently been acquired by Shamrock. *David Donati*

CYRIL EVANS

Cyril Evans Ltd, Cwmparc Garage, Senghenydd, Caerphilly   CF8 2GY

OMA503V	Leyland Leopard PSU3E/4R	Duple Dominant II Express	C49F	1979	Ex Crosville, 1990
MAP340W	Leyland Leopard PSU3F/4R	Plaxton Supreme IV Express	C53F	1981	Ex Brighton & Hove, 1990
MAP341W	Leyland Leopard PSU3F/4R	Plaxton Supreme IV Express	C53F	1981	Ex Fowler, Holbeach Drove, 1990
MAP342W	Leyland Leopard PSU3F/4R	Plaxton Supreme IV Express	C53F	1981	Ex Fowler, Holbeach Drove, 1990
HIW679	Leyland Tiger TRCTL11/3R	Plaxton Supreme V	C57F	1982	
474CUH	Leyland Tiger TRCTL11/3R	Plaxton Paramount 3200	C57F	1983	
EEU359	Leyland Tiger TRCTL11/3R	Plaxton Paramount 3200	C57F	1984	
C262AWR	Leyland Tiger TRCTL11/3R	Plaxton Paramount 3500 II	C53F	1985	Ex Truman's, Pontypool, 1996
JIB506	DAF MB230DKFL615	Plaxton Paramount 3500 III	C51FT	1987	
UIJ742	Leyland Tiger TRCTL11/3ARZ	Duple 340	C53FT	1989	
SIJ408	Leyland Tiger TRCL10/3ARZM	Plaxton Paramount 3500 III	C49FT	1989	Ex Hill's of Tredegar, 1991
H258GRY	Leyland Tiger TR2R62C21Z5/8	Plaxton Paramount 3500 III	C53F	1991	Ex Hellyers, Fareham, 1994
H58GLP	Mercedes-Benz 410D	Premier	M15	1991	Ex van, 1994
J783KHD	DAF SB3000DKV601	Van Hool Alizée	C51FT	1992	Ex Coupland, Rossall, 1993
J832KHD	DAF SB3000DKV601	Van Hool Alizée	C51FT	1992	Ex Coupland, Rossall, 1993
L217ETG	MAN 11-190	Caetano Algarve II	C35F	1994	
N825NUH	Mercedes-Benz 711D	Plaxton Beaver	C25F	1995	

Previous Registrations:

474CUH	A852VHB	HIW679	MUH422X	SIJ408	F595BTG
EEU359	A862WTX	JIB506	E921SNY	UIJ742	F254CDW

Livery: Cream, red and maroon or cream, red and green.

The Cyril Evans coach fleet presently comprises Leyland Leopards, Tigers and a trio of DAFs, the newest of which are a pair of Van Hool Alizee bodied SB3000s acquired from Coupland of Rossall near Blackpool. One of these is J832KHD, seen on a private hire duty in Wood Street, Cardiff.
John Jones

DIAMOND GLANTAWE

D Coaches Ltd, Glantawe Enterprises Ltd, 98 Woodfield Street, Morriston,
Swansea, SA6 6HE

Depot :Plot 15, Duffryn Close, Swansea Enterprise Park, Morriston

ACY62D	Leyland Atlantean PDR1/1	Alexander A	H43/31F	1966	Ex Stevensons, 1985
JSC884E	Leyland Atlantean PDR1/1	Alexander A	H43/31F	1967	Ex West Wales, Tycroes, 1984
YTE113H	Leyland Leopard PSU3A/2R	East Lancashire	B51F	1970	Ex Duff, Sutton-on-the-Forest, 1985
YTE115H	Leyland Leopard PSU3A/2R	East Lancashire	B51F	1970	Ex Duff, Sutton-on-the-Forest, 1985
NTD118K	Leyland Leopard PSU3B/2R	Pennine	B51F	1972	Ex Lancaster, 1981
GHJ384L	Daimler Fleetline CRL6-33	Northern Counties	H49/31D	1972	Ex Glantawe Coaches, Pontardawe, 1995
HGD869L	Leyland Atlantean AN68/1R	Alexander AL	H45/29F	1973	Ex Eynon, Trimsaran, 1984
FUS169L	Leyland Atlantean AN68/1R	Alexander AL	H45/29F	1973	Ex West Wales, Tycroes, 1984
NGB103M	Leyland Atlantean AN68/1R	Alexander AL	H45/29F	1973	Ex Independent, Horsforth, 1985
YBX469M	Leyland Leopard PSU3B/4R	Plaxton Derwent	B51F	1974	Ex Rees & Williams, Tycroes, 1988
HNU125N	Leyland Leopard PSU3B/2R	Duple Dominant	DP53F	1975	Ex Maidstone, 1983
GHM802N	Daimler Fleetline CRL6	MCW	H45/28D	1975	Ex London Transport, 1985
GHM829N	Daimler Fleetline CRL6	MCW	H44/27D	1975	Ex London Transport, 1985
GHM880N	Daimler Fleetline CRL6	MCW	H45/28D	1975	Ex Ensign Bus, Purfleet, 1985
GHV48N	Daimler Fleetline CRL6	Park Royal	H45/28D	1975	Ex Ensign Bus, Purfleet, 1987
GHV52N	Daimler Fleetline CRL6	Park Royal	H45/28D	1975	Ex Dulieu, Ilford, 1985
GHV59N	Daimler Fleetline CRL6	Park Royal	H45/28D	1975	Ex Ensign Bus, Purfleet, 1987
GHV114N	Daimler Fleetline CRL6	Park Royal	H45/28D	1975	Ex Ensign Bus, Purfleet, 1987
LAX72P	Bedford YRQ	Plaxton Supreme III	C45F	1975	Ex Glantawe Coaches, Pontardawe, 1995
KUC144P	Daimler Fleetline CRL6	Park Royal	H45/28D	1975	Ex Peake, Pontypool, 1987
KUC222P	Daimler Fleetline CRL6	MCW	H44/27D	1976	Ex Glantawe Coaches, Pontardawe, 1995
KUC237P	Daimler Fleetline CRL6	MCW	H44/32F	1975	Ex South Wales, 1986
KJD11P	Leyland Fleetline FE30ALR	MCW	H44/32F	1976	Ex South Wales, 1986
KWN815P	Leyland Leopard PSU3C/4R	Plaxton Supreme III Express	DP53F	1976	Ex Rees & Williams, Tycroes, 1988
794YKM	Leyland Leopard PSU3E/4R	Plaxton Viewmaster IV	C53F	1977	Ex Vale of Llangollen, 1986
IIJ5426	Leyland Leopard PSU5B/4R	Plaxton Supreme IV	C53F	1977	Ex Glantawe Coaches, Pontardawe, 1995
VFH700S	Leyland Leopard PSU3C/4R	Duple Dominant I	C53F	1977	Ex Ffoshelig Motors, Newchurch, 1985
UIB3987	Bedford YMT	Plaxton Supreme IV	C53F	1978	Ex Rees & Williams, Tycroes, 1988
ACY51D	Leyland Leopard PSU3E/4R	Plaxton Supreme IV Express	C53F	1979	Ex Rees & Williams, Tycroes, 1988
FUT181V	Dennis Dominator DD120	East Lancashire	H46/33F	1980	Ex Leicester Citybus, 1996
FUT186V	Dennis Dominator DD120	East Lancashire	H46/33F	1980	Ex Leicester Citybus, 1996
MUT253V	Dennis Dominator DD120	East Lancashire	H46/33F	1981	Ex Leicester Citybus, 1996
MUT254V	Dennis Dominator DD120	East Lancashire	H46/33F	1981	Ex Leicester Citybus, 1996
MUT255V	Dennis Dominator DD120	East Lancashire	H46/33F	1981	Ex Leicester Citybus, 1996
MUT261V	Dennis Dominator DD120	East Lancashire	H46/33F	1980	Ex Leicester Citybus, 1996
MUT262V	Dennis Dominator DD120	East Lancashire	H46/33F	1981	Ex Leicester Citybus, 1996
MUT263V	Dennis Dominator DD120	East Lancashire	H46/33F	1980	Ex Leicester Citybus, 1996
ACY50D	Leyland Leopard PSU3E/4R	Plaxton Supreme IV Express	C53F	1981	Ex Rees & Williams, Tycroes, 1988
RIW4963	DAF MB200DKTL600	Plaxton Supreme IV	C50F	1981	Ex Glantawe Coaches, Pontardawe, 1995
581BXP	Volvo B10M-61	Plaxton Viewmaster IV	C51F	1981	Ex Glantawe Coaches, Pontardawe, 1995
TJI6320	DAF MB200DKTL600	Jonckheere Bermuda	C53FT	1982	Ex Glantawe Coaches, Pontardawe, 1995
MCY839X	Leyland Tiger TRCTL11/2R	Plaxton Supreme V Express	C53F	1982	Ex Rees & Williams, Tycroes, 1988
UKE827X	Leyland Leopard PSU3G/4R	Eastern Coach Works B51	C49F	1982	Ex Lancaster, 1993
WAO644Y	Leyland Tiger TRCTL11/2R	Alexander TE	C49F	1983	Ex Lancaster, 1993
LIL7493	DAF MB200DKTL600	Caetano Alpha	C49FT	1983	Ex Glantawe Coaches, Pontardawe, 1995
SIW2763	DAF MB200DKFL600	Caetano Algarve	C50FT	1984	Ex Glantawe Coaches, Pontardawe, 1995
HIL8914	Leyland Tiger TRCTL11/3RH	Duple 340	C49FT	1985	Ex Lancaster, 1993
IIL6234	Volvo B10M-61	Caetano Algarve	C49FT	1986	Ex Jason's, St Mary Cray, 1993
IIL6235	Volvo B10M-61	Caetano Algarve	C49FT	1986	Ex Jason's, St Mary Cray, 1993
D233PWN	Ford Transit VE6	Ford	M12	1987	Ex Glantawe Coaches, Pontardawe, 1995
E647TOJ	Ford Transit VE6	Ford	M14	1988	Ex Glantawe Coaches, Pontardawe, 1995
JIL3585	Volvo B10M-60	Jonckheere Deauville P599	C51FT	1989	Ex Glantawe Coaches, Pontardawe, 1995
JIL3586	Volvo B10M-60	Jonckheere Deauville P599	C51FT	1990	Ex Glantawe Coaches, Pontardawe, 1995
G738LEP	Leyland-DAF 400	Crystals	M16	1990	Ex Glantawe Coaches, Pontardawe, 1995

After purchasing a trio of Dennis Javelins, and several batches of DAFs, the 1996 intake of new coaches for Diamond Glantawe has seen a switch to Volvo B10Ms. N717CYC is one of four similar vehicles which are also notable in being the first Van Hool bodies for this operator. Four more are due in 1997. *Byron Gage*

Diamond Glantawe operates a sizeable fleet of double deckers for use on school contracts in the Swansea area. The oldest vehicles used on this work are Alexander bodied Leyland Atlanteans dating from 1966 to 1973. One of the newest is FUS169L which started life with Glasgow Corporation just before it became a PTE. *Byron Gage*

The most numerous Diamond Glantawe double deckers are the ten Daimler Fleetline CRL6s bodied by MCW or Park Royal and originating with London Transport. GHV48N, a Park Royal example, is seen returning through the Swansea Enterprise Park from Bishop Gore school. *John Jones*

Reg	Chassis	Body	Layout	Year	Notes
K486BCY	DAF SB3000DKV601	Caetano Algarve II	C49FT	1992	
K487BCY	DAF SB3000DKV601	Caetano Algarve II	C49FT	1992	
K537CWN	DAF SB3000DKVF601	Caetano Algarve II	C49FT	1993	
K538CWN	DAF SB3000DKVF601	Caetano Algarve II	C49FT	1993	
K539CWN	DAF SB3000DKVF601	Caetano Algarve II	C49FT	1993	
K540CWN	DAF SB3000DKVF601	Caetano Algarve II	C49FT	1993	
M346MCY	Dennis Javelin 12SDA2134	Berkhof Excellence 1000L	C50FT	1994	
M347MCY	Dennis Javelin 12SDA2134	Berkhof Excellence 1000L	C50FT	1994	
M348MCY	Dennis Javelin 12SDA2134	Berkhof Excellence 1000L	C50FT	1994	
M717NCY	MAN 18.370HOCL	Berkhof Excellence 1000LD	C50FT	1994	Ex Glantawe Coaches, Pontardawe, 1995
N714CYC	Volvo B10M-62	Van Hool Alizée	C48FT	1996	
N715CYC	Volvo B10M-62	Van Hool Alizée	C48FT	1996	
N716CYC	Volvo B10M-62	Van Hool Alizée	C48FT	1996	
N717CYC	Volvo B10M-62	Van Hool Alizée	C48FT	1996	

Previous Registrations:

581BXP	ORR424W	JIL3585	G841GNV
794YKM	RVJ724S, 6052VT, 7239VT	JIL3586	G649ONH
ACY50D	GWN556W	LIL7493	RTH102Y, GJM881
ACY51D	BWN434V	RIW4963	GWN909W, 6927LJ
ACY62D	EWS819D, ACY47D, ACY51D, ACY60D	RIW4964	C411LRP, GJ7698
HIL8914	C76KLG	SIW2763	9309ML
IIJ5426	PCN348R	TJI6320	WRX28X, 146DAF
IIL6234	C683KDS	UIB3987	WTH638T, LFE766
IIL6235	C685KDS		

Livery: Cream and maroon; cream, maroon, red and gold or cream, maroon and blue

For several years, front line coaching duties for Diamond Glantawe were undertaken by Caetano Algarve bodied DAFs such as K538CWN, seen here in Cardiff for a rugby match. Although now three years old, this view confirms the first class condition in which these coaches are presented.
David Donati

After relying on DAF for its frontline coaches three Dennis Javelins arrived in 1994. These carry Berkhof Excellence bodies and were the first from this coachbuilder to be purchased. Since the acquisition of the Glantawe Coaches business in 1995 the company is now a pre-dominant coach operator in south Wales. One the Javelins, M348MCY was photographed in Park Lane, London.
Colin Lloyd

EAST END

R J Jones & Sons Ltd, East End Garage, 5 Pontardawe Road, Clydach,
Neath & Port Talbot   SA6 5NT

ERC882J	Bedford YRQ	Plaxton Elite II	C41F	1971	Ex Trent, 1978
ERC883J	Bedford YRQ	Plaxton Elite II	C41F	1971	Ex Trent, 1978
XRD23K	Bristol VRT/LL2/6LX	Northern Counties	H47/30D	1971	Ex Stevensons, 1983
RHG314K	Seddon RU	Seddon	B46F	1972	Ex Burnley & Pendle, 1982
STJ847L	Seddon RU	Seddon	B51F	1972	Ex Fylde, 1982
STJ850L	Seddon RU	Seddon	B51F	1972	Ex Fylde, 1982
WHN462M	Seddon RU	Pennine	B47D	1973	Ex Darlington, 1991
WHN463M	Seddon RU	Pennine	B47D	1973	Ex Darlington, 1991
WHN468M	Seddon RU	Pennine	B47D	1974	Ex Darlington, 1991
HBD165N	Bristol VRT/SL2/6LX	Eastern Coach Works	H43/31F	1975	Ex United Counties, 1989
HBD166N	Bristol VRT/SL2/6LX	Eastern Coach Works	H43/31F	1975	Ex United Counties, 1989
HDL410N	Bristol VRT/SL2/6LX	Eastern Coach Works	H39/31F	1975	Ex Southern Vectis, 1990
OVV847R	Bristol VRT/SL3/6LXB	Eastern Coach Works	H43/31F	1976	Ex United Counties, 1991
RRP861R	Bristol VRT/SL3/6LXB	Eastern Coach Works	H43/31F	1977	Ex United Counties, 1991
SBA201R	Bedford YMT	Plaxton Supreme III	C52F	1977	Ex Lakeland, Hurst Green, 1994
RPR715R	Bristol VRT/SL3/6LXB	Eastern Coach Works	H43/31F	1977	Ex Solent Blue Line, 1995
VPR489S	Bristol VRT/SL3/6LXB	Eastern Coach Works	H43/31F	1977	Ex Solent Blue Line, 1995
VNH156W	Leyland Leopard PSU3F/4R	Duple Dominant IV	C49F	1981	Ex United Counties, 1991

Livery: Green and cream (buses); white and blue (coaches)

**East End is an operator with extensive schools contracts in the Swansea Valley for which an
interesting bus fleet is maintained. All eight double deckers are Bristol VRTs including OVV847R, a
1976 example acquired from United Counties and seen with a full load near Ystalyfera.** *John Jones*

Edwards Coaches operates what is probably the biggest Leyland Atlantean fleet in Wales with twenty two examples new between 1967 and 1975. Two of them are bodied by East Lancashire, one was originally at Eastbourne, and STD179L, the older of the two, new to Fishwick, Leyland is seen at Tynant near Beddau in May 1996. *John Jones*

The Edwards Coaches fleet contains a great variety of vehicles with most of the chassis makes available over the last twenty years being represented. They include several DAFs such as SOI196, whose modern and well kept appearance belies the fact that it dates from as far back as 1983. *Byron Gage*

EDWARDS COACHES

M C Edwards & P J Ryan; P J Ryan, Newtown Ind Est, Llantwit Fardre,
Rhondda Cynon Taff, CF38 2EE
Grays Coaches Ltd, The Coach Depot, Maritime Ind Est, Pontypridd,
Rhondda Cynon Taff, CF37 1NY

FRJ243D	Leyland Titan PD2/40	Metro Cammell	H36/28F	1966	Ex Powell, Church Village, 1990
MUS281F	Leyland Atlantean PDR1/1	Alexander A	H44/34F	1967	Ex Street, Barnstaple, 1985
ORU236G	Leyland Atlantean PDR1A/1	Alexander A	H43/31F	1969	Ex Mainline, Tonyrefail, 1984
WTN647H	Leyland Atlantean PDR2/1	Alexander J	H48/30D	1969	Ex Mainline, Tonyrefail, 1984
PDW99H	Leyland Atlantean PDR1A/1	Alexander A	H43/31F	1970	Ex K&P John, Llanharry, 1985
PAG760H	Leyland Atlantean PDR1A/1	Alexander J	H45/30D	1970	Ex Rennies, Dunfermline, 1986
TDW315J	Leyland Atlantean PDR1A/1	Alexander J	H43/31F	1971	Ex Taff-Ely, 1987
TDW318J	Leyland Atlantean PDR1A/1	Alexander J	H43/31F	1971	Ex Taff-Ely, 1987
ULJ252J	Leyland Atlantean PDR1A/1	Alexander J	H43/31F	1971	Ex Cyril Evans, Senghenydd, 1990
ULJ253J	Leyland Atlantean PDR1A/1	Alexander J	H43/31F	1971	Ex Cyril Evans, Senghenydd, 1994
ULJ260J	Leyland Atlantean PDR1A/1	Alexander J	H43/31F	1971	Ex Thomas, Clydach Vale, 1989
ULJ264J	Leyland Atlantean PDR1A/1	Alexander J	H43/31F	1971	Ex Thomas, Clydach Vale, 1992
BPA342K	Leyland Atlantean PDR2/1	Alexander L	H49/31D	1971	Ex Thomas, West Ewell, 1994
XRU281K	Leyland Atlantean PDR1A/1	Alexander J	H43/31F	1972	Ex Cyril Evans, Senghenydd, 1994
VNB173L	Leyland Atlantean AN68/1R	Northern Counties	H43/32F	1972	Ex Finglands, 1995
XJA515L	Leyland Atlantean AN68/1R	Park Royal	H43/32F	1972	Ex Finglands, 1995
WBN981L	Leyland Atlantean AN68/1R	Park Royal	H43/32F	1973	Ex Yorkshire Rider, 1991
VNB157L	Leyland Atlantean AN68/1R	Park Royal	H43/32F	1973	Ex Finglands, 1995
STD179L	Leyland Atlantean AN68/1R	East Lancashire	H43/31F	1973	Ex Rennies, Dunfermline, 1986
TRT95M	Leyland Atlantean AN68/1R	Roe	H43/33F	1974	Ex Dining Bus, Bramford, 1994
GHC521N	Leyland Atlantean AN68/1R	East Lancashire	H43/32F	1975	Ex Harris Bus, West Thurrock, 1991
GDB174N	Leyland Atlantean AN68/1R	Northern Counties	H43/32F	1975	Ex East Kent, 1989
HNB40N	Leyland Atlantean AN68/1R	Northern Counties	H43/32F	1975	Ex East Kent, 1989
LMB909P	Bedford VAS5	Duple Dominant	C29F	1976	Ex Gray's, Pontypridd, 1995
PPH432R	AEC Reliance 6U2R	Plaxton Supreme III Express	C49F	1977	Ex Barry Youth Centre, 1993
SDD141R	Leyland Leopard PSU3E/4R	Plaxton Supreme III	C53F	1977	Ex Jervis Bros, Margam, 1994
YAW844T	Bedford YMT	Plaxton Supreme III Express	C53F	1979	Ex East Glam, Nelson, 1989
CAC770T	Bedford VAS5	Duple Dominant	C29F	1978	Ex Ardenvale, Knowle, 1994
YKG53	DAF MB200DKL600	Plaxton Supreme IV	C57F	1979	Ex Mayfayre, Pontypridd, 1986
219LUO	Volvo B58-56	Plaxton Supreme IV Express	C53F	1979	Ex Cambrian, Trebanog, 1989
FEL11V	Leyland Leopard PSU3E/4R	Plaxton Supreme IV Express	C53F	1979	Ex Eagle, Bristol, 1994
LPP347V	Ford R1114	Duple Dominant II	C53F	1980	Ex Thomas, Clydach Vale, 1990
FUJ900V	Ford R1114	Duple Dominant II	C53F	1980	Ex Bebb, Llantwit Fardre, 1987
NRO266V	Ford R1014	Duple Dominant II	C35F	1980	Ex Gray's, Pontypridd, 1995
PWL939W	Leyland Leopard PSU3F/5R	Plaxton Supreme IV Express	C53F	1981	Ex Gray's, Pontypridd, 1995
GTX756W	Bristol VRT/SL3/501	Eastern Coach Works	H43/31F	1980	Ex Rhondda, 1992
MRJ102W	Leyland Leopard PSU5D/5R	Plaxton Supreme IV	C49F	1981	Ex SUT, Dinnington, 1991
XHR104	Volvo B10M-61	Van Hool Alizée	C40FT	1981	Ex Byron's, Skewen, 1992
SND293X	Leyland Leopard PSU5C/4R	Plaxton Supreme V	C57F	1981	Ex Wessex, 1989
SND295X	Leyland Leopard PSU5C/4R	Plaxton Supreme V	C53F	1981	Ex Wessex, 1989
MCY111X	Leyland Leopard PSU5E/4R	Duple Dominant IV	C57F	1982	Ex Brewers, 1994
NTH162X	Leyland Leopard PSU5E/4R	Duple Dominant IV	C53FT	1982	Ex Brewers, 1994
MKH678A	Leyland Leopard PSU5E/4R	Duple Dominant IV	C57F	1982	Ex Brewers, 1994
MKH690A	Leyland Leopard PSU5E/4R	Duple Dominant IV	C57F	1982	Ex Brewers, 1994
MKH730A	Leyland Leopard PSU5E/4R	Duple Dominant IV	C57F	1982	Ex Brewers, 1994
MKH824A	Leyland Leopard PSU5E/4R	Duple Dominant IV	C53FT	1982	Ex Brewers, 1994
SOI196	DAF MB200DKFL600	Jonckheere Jubilee P50	C53FT	1983	Ex Martin, Spean Bridge, 1992
AEF32Y	Bova EL26/581	Bova Europa	C53F	1983	Ex Gray's, Pontypridd, 1995
978HHT	DAF MB200DKFL600	Plaxton Paramount 3200	C50FT	1984	Ex Cambrian, Trebanog, 1988
YAP104	DAF MB200DKVL600	Jonckheere Jubilee P50	C53F	1985	Ex Roman City, Bath, 1986
B221OJU	Bedford YNT	Duple Laser	C53F	1983	Ex Gray's, Pontypridd, 1995
SJI2449	Leyland Tiger TRCTL11/3RH(Vo)	Plaxton Paramount 3500 II	C51FT	1986	Ex Rhondda, 1992
210HKT	Leyland Tiger TRCTL11/3RH(Vo)	Van Hool Alizée	C48FT	1986	Ex Thomas, Clydach Vale, 1988
C598HTX	DAF MB200DKFL600	Plaxton Paramount 3200 II	C57F	1986	Ex Humphreys, Pontypridd, 1993

Coaches confined mainly to contract work in the Edwards Coaches fleet are painted in a simple but not unattractive cream livery with blue lettering. A relatively recent addition is FEL11V, a Plaxton Supreme Express bodied Leyland Leopard, new to Bournemouth, and seen approaching Efail Isaf.
John Jones

E321TTX	DAF MB230LB615	Plaxton Paramount 3200 III	C55F	1988	Ex Humphreys, Pontypridd, 1994
F575KVL	Freight Rover Sherpa	Howells	M16	1988	Ex Gray's, Pontypridd, 1995
LIL9407	Bova FHD12.290	Bova Futura	C49FT	1989	Ex Transcity, Crockenhill, 1996
MIL2407	Bova FHD12.290	Bova Futura	C49FT	1989	Ex Transcity, Crockenhill, 1996
G416WFP	Bova FHD12.290	Bova Futura	C48FT	1990	Ex Boyden, Castle Donington, 1991
J292TTX	Ford Transit	Ford	M14	1991	
M542JHB	Bova FHD12.340	Bova Futura	C53FT	1994	
M720LTG	Toyota Coaster HZB50R	Caetano Optimo III	C21F	1995	

Previous Registrations:

210HKT	C334HHB		MKH824A	MCY113X
219LUO	BWN811V, 978HHT, GHB197V		NTH162X	MCY112X, DDZ1213
978HHT	A546XUH		PWL939W	LWL745W, VWL817
BPA342K	XKC816K, V649MAN		SJI2449	C262GUH
LIL9407	F261NUT		SOI106	NNV608Y
MIL2407	F262NUT		XHR104	TGD765W
MKH678A	MCY115X		YAP104	B495CBD
MKH690A	MCY116X		YKG53	HRO445V
MKH730A	MCY114X			

Livery: Cream and blue (Edwards) cream and orange (Grays)

The majority of Edwards Coaches Leyland Atlanteans are bodied by Alexander and six of them were originally owned by Bournemouth Transport. ULJ264J is one of four from the same batch and is seen on the busy Bridgend to Pontypridd road at Church Village. *John Jones*

Edwards Coaches newest vehicle is M720LTG, a Toyota Coaster with Caetano Optimo III bodywork, which gets well away from the converted van image and provides quality transport for parties too small to warrant use of a full size coach which, in the Edwards example, would probably be a Bova Futura. *Robert Edworthy*

EXPRESS MOTORS

VI & DV Evans, 37 Commercial Street, Kenfig Hill, Bridgend CF33 6DH

HRN923N	Ford R1014	Duple Dominant	C45F	1975	Ex GM, Cefn Cribwr, 1982
ECA160S	Ford R1114	Plaxton Supreme III	C53F	1978	Ex Childs, Kiveton Park, 1992
MMB145T	Ford R1114	Plaxton Supreme IV Express	C53F	1979	Ex Fisher, Bronington, 1994
EWW219T	Leyland Leopard PSU3E/4R	Duple Dominant II	C53F	1979	Ex Burton, Fellbeck, 1988
BCY383V	Ford R1114	Duple Dominant II	C53F	1979	
LUA263V	Ford R1114	Plaxton Supreme IV	C53F	1980	Ex Stevens, Bristol, 1993
RMB403V	Ford R1114	Plaxton Supreme IV	C53F	1980	Ex Mellisham Coaches, 1995
EYA251X	DAF MB200DKFL600	Plaxton Supreme V	C53F	1982	Ex Bailey, Biddisham, 1992
A724FRM	DAF SB2300DHS585	Plaxton Paramount 3200	C53F	1984	Ex Robinson's, Appleby, 1991
A707YKG	Volvo B10M-56	Plaxton Paramount 3200E	C53F	1984	

Previous Registrations:

A724FRM	990ENR		EYA251X	BYC990X, 28XYB

Livery: Lilac and cerise

Heavyweight coaches are in the minority in the Express fleet where the Ford R1114 is still providing reliable service. The heavyweights include a couple of DAFs, one of which is a rear engined SB model which, as this view of A724FRM shows, is fitted with Plaxton Paramount coachwork. *John Jones*

FERRIS HOLIDAYS

K Ferris and S G Owen, Universal Garage, Commercial Street,
Senghenydd, Caerphilly   CF8 2GY
R Ferris, The Coach Yard, Cardiff Road, Nantgarw, Cardiff CF4 7SR

MKH748A	Leyland Leopard PSU5C/4R	Duple Dominant II	C51F	1979	Ex Brewers, 1991
DGS681X	Mercedes-Benz 0303	Jonckheere Jubilee	C40FT	1982	Ex Cantabrica, Watford, 1991
XSV695	Scania K112CRS	Van Hool Alizée	C49FT	1984	Ex Contact Coaches, Aberdare, 1992
NJI3995	Scania K112TRB	Jonckheere Jubilee P90	CH55/18CT	1988	Ex Mercer's, Grimsargh, 1992
E753NGA	Hestair Duple SDA1512	Duple 425	C50FT	1988	Ex Wilson, Blaydon, 1991
F871CNY	Hestair Duple SDA1512	Duple 425	C53FT	1989	
F623CWJ	Aüwaerter Neoplan N122/3	Aüwaerter Skyliner	CH58/22CT	1989	Ex Channel Coachways, Bow, 1994
F631CWJ	Aüwaerter Neoplan N122/3	Aüwaerter Skyliner	CH58/22CT	1989	Ex Mayo, Caterham, 1993
F223RJX	DAF SBR3000DKZ570	Plaxton Paramount 4000 III	CH55/19CT	1989	Ex Cosgroves, Preston, 1994
F224RJX	DAF SBR3000DKZ570	Plaxton Paramount 4000 III	CH55/19CT	1989	Ex Cosgroves, Preston, 1994
G120AAD	Volvo B10M-60	Ikarus Blue Danube	C49FT	1989	Ex Applegates, Newport (Glos), 1994
J42VWO	Volvo B10M-60	Plaxton Paramount 3500 III	C51FT	1992	Ex Bebb, Llantwit Fardre, 1995
J43VWO	Volvo B10M-60	Plaxton Paramount 3500 III	C51FT	1992	Ex Bebb, Llantwit Fardre, 1995
L544XUT	Volvo B10M-60	Jonckheere Deauville 45	C51FT	1993	
L351YNR	Dennis Javelin 12SDA2125	Plaxton Premiére 350	C53FT	1993	
L218ETG	Dennis Javelin 12SDA2134	Berkhof Excellence 1000	C50FT	1994	
M303KRY	Volvo B10M-62	Jonckheere Deauville 45	C51FT	1995	
N595DWY	DAF DE33WSSB3000	Van Hool Alizée	C51FT	1995	
N827XRD	DAF DE33WSSB3000	Berkhof Excellence 1000	C51FT	1996	

Previous Registrations:

DGS681X	ENV833X, TSV804		NJI3995	E214GNV
MKH748A	GDF281V		XSV695	B189VPP

Livery: White, orange, yellow and red

The Ferris Holidays fleet is anything but standard with no less than eight chassis and six body makers products included in a complement of nineteen coaches. The latest acquisitions are DAF SB3000s, one of which, N595DWY, is fitted with timelessly attractive Van Hool Alizée bodywork. *Byron Gage*

GM of Cefn Cribbwr's OIB7915 is one of three Berkhof Esprite bodied Volvo B10Ms in this small fleet. Two of them, including this one, which was registered A632SKK when new, originated in the well established, Kent-based fleet, The Kings Ferry. *Byron Gage*

Gavenny Bus operates minibuses out of a yard at Lion Street, Abergavenny, including a pair of Dormobile converted Freight Rover Sherpas new to Badgerline and acquired via Phil Anslow two years ago. D574EWS, with D583EWS behind, are seen when taking a break from the Abergavenny town service. *John Jones*

G M

R G Millington, Mountain View Garage, Tyfry Road, Cefn Cribwr
Bridgend CF32 0BB

MCO253H	Leyland Atlantean PDR2/1	Park Royal	H49/32D	1970	Ex Light, East Stour, 1989
UKE416H	Leyland Leopard PSU4A/4R	Marshall	B45F	1970	Ex Maidstone & District, 1982
WKE69S	Bedford YMT	Duple Dominant	B61F	1978	Ex Roberts Cs, Maerdy, 1994
AKK174T	Bedford YMT	Duple Dominant	B61F	1978	Ex Roberts Cs, Maerdy, 1994
UHW10T	Leyland Leopard PSU3E/4R	Plaxton Supreme IV	C53F	1978	Ex Blue Iris, Nailsea, 1993
OIB5880	Volvo B10M-61	Berkhof Esprite 350	C49FT	1983	Ex Brixham Travel, 1993
OIB7915	Volvo B10M-61	Berkhof Esprite 350	C53F	1984	Ex The King's Ferry, 1989
OIB7631	Volvo B10M-61	Berkhof Esprite 340	C53F	1984	Ex The King's Ferry, 1991

Previous Registrations:

OIB5880	ADV147Y, A144JTA, 755HWP, A942RTT
OIB7631	A581RVW, 951JNU, A973SKK
OIB7915	A576RVW, 279NDE, A632SKK

Livery: Beige and red

GAVENNY BUS

G & K R Lewis, 1 Trinity Terrace, Baker Street, Abergavenny, Monmouthshire, NP7 5BE

Depot :Horsington's Yard, Lion Street, Abergavenny

B654ETG	Freight Rover Sherpa	Freight Rover	M12	1984	Ex MoD, 1993
D574EWS	Freight Rover Sherpa	Dormobile	B16F	1986	Ex Phil Anslow Travel, Garndiffaith, 1994
D583EWS	Freight Rover Sherpa	Dormobile	B16F	1986	Ex Phil Anslow Travel, Garndiffaith, 1994
D212MBO	Bedford CFL	Dormobile	M16	1986	Ex Mid Glamorgan CC, 1992

Livery White and blue

Glyn Williams services were, in the early post-deregulation years, operated by a couple of Bristol REs, Leyland Leopards and a few coaches. These were gradually replaced by Mercedes-Benz midibuses on suitable routes and by Leyland Nationals. Now the Leyland Nationals have themselves been largely displaced by more-recent Leyland National 2s such as 29, LRB200W, caught by the camera in mid U-turn at the refurbished Newport bus station. *John Jones*

The latest midibuses for Glyn Williams are once again based on Mercedes-Benz chassis, 811Ds with Plaxton Beaver bodywork. One of the trio new in 1994 is 27, M242JHB, seen arriving at Newport bus station. *Richard Godfrey*

GLYN WILLIAMS

G J, F J & T G Williams, Risca House, Waunfawr Gardens, Crosskeys, Caerphilly NP1 7BL
Crosskeys Coach Hire Ltd, Pennar Halt Garage, Pentwynmawr,
Pontllanfraith, Caerphilly NP2 2AW

Depot : Pennar Halt Garage, Pentwynmawr

1	RSG821V	Leyland National 2 NL116L11/1R		B52F	1979	Ex Weir, Clydebank, 1995
3	YSX927W	Leyland National 2 NL106L11/1R		B44F	1980	Ex Weir, Clydebank, 1995
4	KDW327P	Leyland National 11351/1R		B49F	1976	Ex National Welsh, 1991
6	L920UGA	Mercedes-Benz 709D	Dormobile Routemaker	B29F	1993	
7	EON827V	Leyland National 2 NL116L11/1R		B49F	1980	Ex Yorkshire Buses, 1994
8	G830UMU	Mercedes-Benz 609D	Reeve Burgess Beaver	B20F	1989	
9	E320OMG	Mercedes-Benz 609D	Reeve Burgess Beaver	B20F	1988	
10	M528KTG	Mercedes-Benz 811D	Plaxton Beaver	B31F	1995	
11	WUH174T	Leyland National 11351A/1R (Volvo)		B49F	1978	Ex Cynon Valley, 1992
14	MHJ721V	Leyland National 2 NL116L11/1R		B52F	1980	Ex Eastern National, 1995
15	K97RGA	Mercedes-Benz 709D	Dormobile Routemaker	B29F	1993	
17	YDW401T	Leyland National 10351A/1R (Volvo)		B44F	1979	Ex Rhondda, 1993
18	HHH371V	Leyland National 2 NL116L11/1R		B52F	1980	Ex Ribble, 1994
19	RSG818V	Leyland National 2 NL116L11/1R		B52F	1979	Ex Weir, Clydebank, 1995
20	MHJ732V	Leyland National 2 NL116L11/1R		B52F	1980	Ex Eastern National, 1994
21	LRB212W	Leyland National 2 NL116AL11/1R		B52F	1981	Ex Yorkshire Buses, 1994
22	CBV790S	Leyland National 11351A/1R (Volvo)		B49F	1977	Ex Thames Transit, 1991
23	MHJ729V	Leyland National 2 NL116L11/1R		B52F	1980	Ex Eastern National, 1995
24	E814XHS	Mercedes Benz 609D	Alexander AM	DP25F	1988	Ex Puma Coaches, Erskine,1994
26	M243JHB	Mercedes-Benz 811D	Plaxton Beaver	B31F	1994	
27	M242JHB	Mercedes-Benz 811D	Plaxton Beaver	B31F	1994	
28	M244JHB	Mercedes-Benz 811D	Plaxton Beaver	B31F	1994	
29	LRB200W	Leyland National 2 NL116L11/1R		B52F	1980	Ex Yorkshire Buses, 1994
30	NAT201V	Leyland National 2 NL116L11/1R		B49F	1980	Ex Yorkshire Buses, 1994
31	LRB216W	Leyland National 2 NL116AL11/1R		B52F	1981	Ex Yorkshire Buses, 1994
	VBG83V	Leyland National 2 NL116L11/1R		B49F	1980	Ex GMN, 1996
	PNW604W	Leyland National 2 NL116L11/1R		B51F	1980	Ex GMN, 1996

Livery: Green and white

Glyn Williams 20,
MHJ732V, is one of
three Leyland
National 2s acquired
from Eastern
National in 1994-95
and is seen passing
through
Pontllanfraith on a
morning run out of
Blackwood. The
Blackwood-Newport
services are now
worked entirely by
this type *John Jones*

The South Wales Bus Handbook

HARRIS

Harris Coaches (Pengam) Ltd, Bryn-Gwyn, Fleur-de-Lys, Blackwood, Caerphilly NP2 1RZ

2	D151NON	Freight Rover Sherpa	Carlyle	B20F	1986	Ex Ribble, 1988
4	D875LWR	Freight Rover Sherpa	Dormobile	B20F	1987	Ex Tame Valley, Birmingham, 1991
5	D418FEH	Freight Rover Sherpa(Ford)	PMT Bursley	B20F	1987	Ex Rainbow Bus, Dunkerswell, 1990
8	C722JJO	Ford Transit 190D	Carlyle	B20F	1986	Ex Oxford Bus Company, 1990
9	C723JJO	Ford Transit 190D	Carlyle	B20F	1986	Ex Oxford Bus Company, 1990
14	YYE273T	Leyland National 10351A/2R		B38D	1978	Ex London Buses, 1990
	THX161S	Leyland National 10351A/2R		B44F	1978	Ex London Buses, 1992
	2375NU	Bova EL26/581	Bova Europa	C53F	1981	Ex Boulton, Cardington, 1986
	2039NU	DAF MB200DKFL600	Caetano Algarve	C52FT	1984	
	D300XCX	DAF SB2300DHTD585	Plaxton Paramount 3200 III	C53F	1987	Ex Silverwing, Keynsham, 1994
	D186PWN	MCW MetroRider MF150/7	MCW	B25F	1987	Ex SWT, 1994
	D257PEP	MCW MetroRider MF150/16	MCW	B25F	1987	Ex SWT, 1994
	E133SNY	MCW MetroRider MF150/52	MCW	B23F	1987	Ex Cardiff Bus, 1995
	E136SNY	MCW MetroRider MF150/52	MCW	B23F	1987	Ex Cardiff Bus, 1995
	E978DGS	MCW MetroRider MF150/72	MCW	B25F	1988	Ex County (Welwyn Hatfield), 1995
	F130YVP	MCW MetroRider MF158/16	MCW	B28F	1988	Ex Stagecoach East London, 1996
	F131YVP	MCW MetroRider MF158/16	MCW	B28F	1988	Ex Stagecoach East London, 1996
	F982EDS	Mercedes-Benz 609D	North West Coach Sales	C24F	1988	Ex Clydeside 2000, 1993
	F757GUS	Mercedes-Benz 609D	Scott	C24F	1989	Ex Clydeside 2000, 1993
	F921MTM	Mercedes-Benz 709D	Robin Hood	B29F	1989	Ex North Mymms, 1991
	F150TRY	DAF SB2305DHS585	Caetano Algarve	C53FT	1989	Ex James Brothers, Llangeitho, 1995
	G34OHS	Mercedes-Benz 609D	North West Coach Sales	C24F	1989	Ex Clydeside 2000, 1993
	G168XJF	DAF SB2305DHS585	Caetano Algarve	C53FT	1990	

Previous Registrations:

2375NU	LBO6X		2039NU	From new		F150TRY	F425RRY, 6738UN

Livery: Cream, maroon and red

Only three Freight Rover Sherpas and a pair of Ford Transits remain of the original Harris stage carriage fleet, the others having been displaced by Mercedes-Benz midibuses and MCW MetroRiders. One of the latter, E978DGS, is seen leaving Caerphilly for Bargoed a service which goes through Gelligaer.
Richard Godfrey

F921MTM, a Mercedes-Benz 709D with Robin Hood bodywork was the first of this chassis make to be acquired by Harris when the need arose for vehicles of larger carrying capacity than the twenty seat Freight Rover Sherpas. It was acquired in 1991 from North Mymms and is seen at Ystrad Mynach. *Byron Gage*

All five Harris coaches, including a Bova Europa, are DAF powered and two were bought new. The first of these, 2039NU, which has carried this dateless index mark since delivery in 1984, is still maintained in fine condition as evidenced by this view taken in Fleur-de-Lys. *John Jones*

Hawkes are based midway between Swansea and Llanelli, at Waunarlwydd, having moved there from Gorseinon shortly after commencing operation in the early 1970s. Apart from a Leyland Leopard owned briefly during 1980, it was 1985 before heavyweight coaches started to enter the fleet in earnest. Volvo was the choice then and that remains the case today as evidenced by *(bottom)* TJI1698 a Van Hool bodied B10M-61. Hawkes commenced stage operations shortly after de-regulation and the Penyrheol to Swansea service is now well established. The former regulars on this route are now replaced by Leyland Nationals including *(top)* THX145S one of two to arrive from Rhondda in 1994. *David Donati/John Jones*

HAWKES

Hawkes Coaches Ltd, The Garage, Bridge Road, Waunarlwydd,
Swansea   SA5 4SP

TDL566K	Bristol RELL6G	Eastern Coach Works	B53F	1972	Ex Atlas, Gorseinon, 1991
BCJ700L	Bedford YRT	Plaxton Elite III	C53F	1973	Ex John, Rogerstone, 1980
UNW10M	Leyland Leopard PSU3B/4R	Plaxton Elite III	C53F	1974	Ex Owen, Oswestry, 1987
JKV104N	Bedford YRT	Duple Dominant	C53F	1975	Ex Nadder Valley, Tisbury, 1981
KVD456P	AEC Reliance 6U3ZR	Duple Dominant	C50F	1975	Ex Knotty Bus, Chesterton, 1993
NNX285P	Bedford YMT	Duple Dominant	C53F	1976	Ex National Travel West, 1979
JTH769P	Leyland National 11351/1R		B52F	1976	Ex Brian Isaac, Morriston, 1995
NSJ4R	Seddon Pennine 7	Alexander AY	B53F	1976	Ex Clydeside Scottish, 1988
SLO513R	Bedford YMT	Duple Dominant	C53F	1977	Ex Pullman, Crofty, 1994
NWO462R	Leyland National 11351A/1R/SC		DP48F	1977	Ex Rhondda, 1994
VAY310S	Bedford YMT	Van Hool McArdle	C49F	1977	Ex Davies Bros, Carmarthen, 1991
OIB8587	Volvo B58-61	Duple Dominant II	C57F	1977	Ex Field, Balby, 1992
THX145S	Leyland National 10351A/2R		B44F	1978	Ex Rhondda, 1994
EFX104T	Volvo B58-61	Plaxton Supreme III	C50FT	1978	Ex Knight's, Cwmllynfell, 1993
VNT49S	Bedford YMT	Duple Dominant II	C53F	1978	Ex Hylton & Dawson, Leicester, 1990
ANY587T	Bedford YMT	Plaxton Supreme IV	C53F	1979	Ex Capitol Coaches, Cwmbran,1981
ULS668T	Leyland Fleetline FE30AGR	Eastern Coach Works	H43/31F	1979	Ex Green Lane, Muswell Hill, 1995
YNY588T	Volvo B58-56	Plaxton Supreme IV Express	C53F	1979	Ex Perry, Slingsby, 1985
EYP30V	Bedford YMT	Plaxton Supreme IV	C53F	1980	Ex Evans, Tregaron, 1995
JNJ365V	Bedford YMT	Duple Dominant II	C53F	1980	Ex Evans, Tregaron, 1995
HJP479V	Volvo B58-61	Duple Dominant II	C53F	1980	Ex Bere Regis & District, 1991
MUE313V	Volvo B58-61	Duple Dominant II	C53F	1980	Ex Bell, New Silksworth, 1992
898FCY	Volvo B58-61	Duple Dominant II	C53F	1980	Ex Bere Regis & District, 1989
JSJ426W	Volvo B10M-61	Duple Dominant II	C53F	1981	Ex Smith, Wigan, 1986
GIL6240	Volvo B58-61	Duple Dominant IV	C53F	1982	Ex Shearings, 1989
GIL6241	Volvo B10M-61	Duple Dominant IV	C50F	1982	Ex National Travel East, 1987
723CTH	Volvo B10M-61	Duple Caribbean	C51F	1984	Ex Reliance, Gravesend, 1989
TJI1698	Volvo B10M-61	Van Hool Alizée	C52FT	1984	Ex Turner, Bristol, 1994
A616WEP	Mercedes-Benz L608D	Reeve Burgess	C25F	1984	Ex Collins, Roch, 1996
C285EHU	Volvo B10M-61	Duple 340	C57F	1986	Ex Turner, Bristol, 1994
C644KDS	Volvo B10M-61	Caetano Algarve	C49FT	1986	Ex Shevill, Carluke, 1994
D967NCY	Bedford CFL	Steedrive Parflo	M12	1987	Ex Briton Ferry Minibus, 1987
E97OUH	Freight Rover Sherpa(Ford)	Carlyle Citybus 2	B20F	1987	Ex Red & White, 1996
E381TEP	Ford Transit VE6	Ford	M14	1988	Ex Merlyn's, Skewen, 1989
E940THB	Ford Transit VE6	Ford	M14	1988	Ex Merlyn's, Skewen, 1989

Previous Registrations:

723CTH	A227LFX	GIL6241	OHE272X
898FCY	HJP481V	JNJ365V	DMT904V, 710VCV
C285EHU	C941DHT, 139MDV	OIB8587	ACK7R,898FCY,PWN759R
EFX104T	OJS30T, CL5561, 4932PH	TJI1698	A637EJS, 2080NT, A682VSK
GIL6240	TND128X		

Livery: White and blue (coaches); yellow and blue (buses)

HAWTHORN

N P Martlew, Gwalia Buildings, Powell Duffryn Way, Barry Docks,   CF62 5QR

Reg	Chassis	Body	Seating	Year	History
DMA515K	Bedford YRQ	Plaxton Elite	C45F	1972	Ex Goodwin, Stockport, 1988
HLJ97N	Ford R1114	Plaxton Elite III	C53F	1975	Ex CK-Bowers, Cardiff, 1991
HBX190N	Bristol LHL6L	Plaxton Elite III	C51F	1975	
PRS517R	Bedford YLQ	Plaxton Supreme III	C45F	1976	Ex Formby Coaches, 1987
NNN399P	Ford R1114	Willowbrook	B53F	1976	Ex Brixham Travel, 1993
SEL128R	Ford R1114	Plaxton Supreme III	C53F	1977	Ex Tedd, Winterslow, 1988
YFR494R	Leyland Leopard PSU3E/4R	Duple Dominant I	C47F	1977	Ex Hazell, Northlew, 1994
VPR863S	Bedford YLQ	Plaxton Supreme III	C41F	1978	Ex Priory Coaches, Gosport, 1994
VVD433S	Bedford YMT	Duple Dominant II	C53F	1978	Ex Poynter, Wye, 1990
GSU9T	AEC Reliance 6U3ZR	Plaxton Supreme III	C51F	1979	Ex Blue Link, Dallington, 1983
BFX745T	Bedford YMT	Plaxton Supreme IV	C53F	1979	Ex Barry's of Weymouth, 1994
VOR579T	Ford R1114	Duple Dominant II	C53F	1979	Ex Priory Coaches, Gosport, 1990
YFB8V	Bedford YMT	Plaxton Supreme IV	C53F	1979	Ex Barry's of Weymouth, 1993
OWU992W	Mercedes-Benz L508D	Whittaker	C21F	1980	Ex Alister's, Barry, 1995
NCX25W	Bedford YMT	Plaxton Supreme IV	C53F	1981	Ex Barnes, Aldbourne, 1995
GFO770X	Bedford YNT	Duple Dominant IV	C53F	1981	Ex Len Hopkins, Ogmore Vale, 1994
BKH301X	Volvo B10M-61	Van Hool Alizée	C49FT	1982	Ex Appleby, Conisholme, 1990
THH287X	Mercedes-Benz L308	Reeve Burgess	M12	1982	Ex Jones International, Llandeilo, 1989
AEX402X	Mercedes-Benz L508D	Devon Conversions	C19F	1982	Ex Melksham Coaches, 1991
FIL8541	Volvo B10M-61	Van Hool Alizée	C49FT	1982	Ex Harris, Summercourt, 1995
KOW66Y	Mercedes-Benz L508DG	Reeve Burgess	C19F	1982	Ex Trueman, Camberley, 1989
OIB6694	Volvo B10M-61	Van Hool Alizée	C49FT	1984	Ex City Central, Bermondsey, 1992
A63OJX	Volvo B10M-61	Duple Laser	C57F	1984	Ex Turner, Bristol, 1992
A500WGF	Volvo B10M-61	Plaxton Paramount 3500	C50F	1984	Ex Epsom Coaches, 1993
JIL2665	Leyland Tiger TRCTL11/3RZ	Plaxton Paramount 3500	C49FT	1984	Ex Harris, Summercourt, 1995
B444OCC	Bedfotd YNT	Duple Laser	C53F	1985	Ex Filer, Ilfacombe, 1990
G844GNV	Volvo B10M-60	Jonckheere Deauville P599	C51F	1989	Ex Hazell, Northlaw, 1994

Previous Registrations:

FIL8541	FGB737X	OIB6694	A847TDS, 784CLC, A171NJK
JIL2665	9616DD, A882GEJ		

Livery: White, tan and brown

Hawthorn has its roots in a minibus business started in 1971 by a Mr Owen. His second vehicle was a Bedford SB13, but despite this the business became the Barry Minibus Co Ltd in 1972, finally Hawthorn Travel Ltd at the end of 1973. In the mid 1980s ownership of the business changed twice and it is now controlled by Nigel Martlew. The fleet is now the largest in Barry and council contracts account for much of the work done. A mixed fleet has been employed including GSU9T a Plaxton bodied AEC Reliance new to Hutchison of Overtown.
David Donati

HENLEY'S

Henley's Bus Services Ltd, 69 Tillery Road, Abertillery, Blaenau Gwent   NP3 1HU

Depot :Victor Road, Abertillery

WKG287	AEC Reliance 2MU3RA	Willowbrook	B41F	1961	Ex Humphries, Bridgend, 1976
OAX500M	AEC Reliance 6MU4R	Plaxton Derwent	B47F	1973	
KJD412P	Bristol LH6L	Eastern Coach Works	B39F	1976	Ex Mair, Bucksburn, 1993
UWO240S	AEC Reliance 6U3ZR	Duple Dominant II	C51F	1978	
GMS282S	Leyland Leopard PSU3E/4R	Alexander AYS	B53F	1978	Ex Kelvin Scottish, 1987
GTG779W	Leyland Leopard PSU3F/5R	Plaxton Supreme IV Express	C51F	1980	
PKG702Y	Leyland Tiger TRCTL11/2R	Plaxton Supreme V	C51F	1982	
C499FAX	Leyland Tiger TRCTL11/2RZ	Duple Laser 2	C51F	1985	
JBZ6925	Leyland Tiger TRCTL11/3RZ	Plaxton Paramount 3500 III	C53F	1986	Ex Vale of Llangollen, 1993
D317UTU	Volvo B10M-61	Plaxton Paramount 3500 III	C51F	1987	Ex Vale of Llangollen, 1996
E185UKG	Freight Rover Sherpa	Carlyle Citybus 2	B20F	1988	Ex Brown, Buith Wells, 1993
M201RHB	Mercedes-Benz 711D	Alexander Sprint	B29F	1995	

Previous Registrations:
D317UTU   D288UDM, VLT280, 3810VT, VLT483
JBZ6925   C710LMA, 7052VT, C736NCA, 440VT, C814NCA

Livery: Green and white (buses), green, white and orange (coaches)

Henleys well-known reliance (!) on AECs for its services around Abertillery have always ensured their appearance in this volume. Times do change, however, and minibuses play an increasing role including this former National Welsh Freight Rover Sherpa E185UKG. *Richard Godfrey*

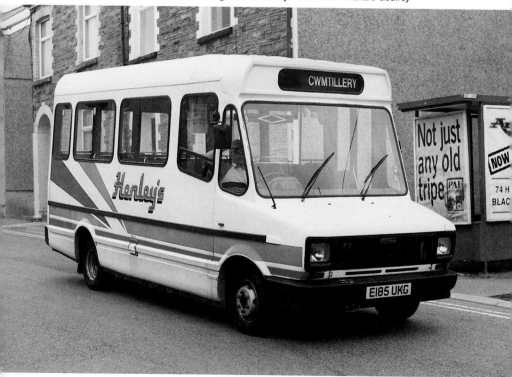

HOWELLS COACHES

REL & P Howells, Ffos-yr-hebog Farm, Deri, Bargoed, Caerphilly   CF8 8NT

Depot :Ffos-yr-hebog Farm, Deri and Nyddfa Garage, Pengam

SBR87P	Ford R1114	Plaxton Supreme III	C53F	1975	Ex Sunline Coaches, Porth, 1995
OJD196R	Leyland Fleetline FE30AGR	MCW	H45/32F	1977	Ex Thamesdown, 1994
OJD234R	Leyland Fleetline FE30AGR	MCW	H45/32F	1977	Ex Thamesdown, 1994
OJD239R	Leyland Fleetline FE30AGR	MCW	H45/32F	1977	Ex Thamesdown, 1994
CFX308T	Ford R1114	Plaxton Supreme IV	C49F	1979	Ex Hurst & Leek, Goose Green, 1994
JDB952V	Ford R1114	Plaxton Supreme IV	C53F	1980	Ex E&J Coaches, Batley, 1994
D108CKV	Renault-Dodge S56	Mellor	B22F	1986	Ex A-tax, Aberbargoed, 1995
D132WCC	Freight Rover Sherpa	Carlyle	B18F	1987	Ex Owen, Oswestry, 1992
F79CJC	Iveco Daily 49.10	Carlyle Dailybus 2	B25F	1988	Ex Crosville Cymru, 1995
F998XOV	Iveco Daily 49.10	Carlyle Dailybus 2	B23F	1989	Ex Bluebird, Middleton, 1995

Previous Registrations:
SBR87P   JAS521P

Livery: various

Roy Howells of
Deri has operated
a double decker
for some years
now but the
arrival of three
London
DMS-type
Fleetlines from
Thamesdown in
1994 was
somewhat of a
surprise. They
had retained their
former operators
livery until this
volume was in
preparation when
one appeared in
all-over red.
However,
OJD234R was
photographed
earlier in the year
near
Llanbradach.
Ian Kirby

I B T

Islwyn Borough Transport Ltd, Penmaen Road, Pontllanfraith, Caerphilly   NP2 1YF

1w	LBO728P	Leyland Leopard PSU4C/2R	Willowbrook	B45F	1976	
02	L4USE	Mercedes-Benz 811D	Dormobile Routemaker	B33F	1993	Ex Patterson, Birmingham, 1995
3	NTX577R	Leyland Leopard PSU4C/2R	Willowbrook	B45F	1976	
04	F852LHS	Mercedes-Benz 811D	Alexander Sprint	DP33F	1989	Ex Kelvin Central, 1995
5	LBO729P	Leyland Leopard PSU4C/2R	Willowbrook	B45F	1976	
06	F349TSX	Mercedes-Benz 811D	Alexander Sprint	DP31F	1988	Ex Kelvin Central, 1995
7w	LBO730P	Leyland Leopard PSU4C/2R	Willowbrook	B45F	1976	
08	F94KDS	Mercedes-Benz 811D	Alexander Sprint	DP33F	1989	Ex Kelvin Central, 1995
09	H907XGA	Mercedes-Benz 814D	Reeve Burgess Beaver	C33F	1990	Ex Kelvin Central, 1995
10	N572OUH	Mercedes-Benz 811D	Plaxton Beaver	B29F	1995	
11	N571OUH	Mercedes-Benz 811D	Plaxton Beaver	B29F	1995	
12	N573OUH	Mercedes-Benz 811D	Plaxton Beaver	B29F	1995	
14	YDW565T	Leyland Leopard PSU4E/2R	Marshall	B45F	1979	
21	UDW939S	Leyland Leopard PSU4E/2R	Willowbrook	B45F	1978	
25	OAX974M	Leyland Leopard PSU4B/2R	Willowbrook	B45F	1973	
27	YDW566T	Leyland Leopard PSU4E/2R	Marshall	B45F	1979	
34	DNY534V	Leyland Leopard PSU4E/2R	Marshall	B45F	1980	
37	GAX137W	Leyland Leopard PSU4F/2R	Marshall	B45F	1981	
41	C41GKG	Leyland Tiger TRBTL11/2RP	East Lancashire	DP47F	1985	
42	C42GKG	Leyland Tiger TRBTL11/2RP	East Lancashire	DP47F	1985	
43	C43GKG	Leyland Tiger TRBTL11/2RP	East Lancashire	DP47F	1985	
44	D44MBO	Leyland Tiger TRBTL11/2RP	East Lancashire	DP47F	1986	
46	D46MBO	Leyland Tiger TRBTL11/2RP	East Lancashire	DP47F	1986	
47	D405NUH	Dodge Commando GO8	East Lancashire	DP25F	1987	
48	D406NUH	Dodge Commando GO8	East Lancashire	DP25F	1987	
50	D408NUH	Dodge Commando GO8	East Lancashire	DP25F	1987	
56	IIL7331	DAF MB230 DKVL600	Caetano Algarve	C53FT	1987	Ex Peter Sheffield, Cleethorpes 1988
64	PHB309R	Leyland Leopard PSU3C/2R	Duple Dominant	B53F	1977	Ex Inter Valley Link, 1989
65	PHB310R	Leyland Leopard PSU3C/2R	Duple Dominant	B53F	1977	Ex Inter Valley Link, 1989
67	KIB1767	Leyland Leopard PSU3E/1/3R	Van Hool Alizée	C46FT	1984	Ex Parfitt's Rhymney Bridge, 1989
68	NIB3214	DAF MB200DKFL600	Jonckheere Jubilee P50	C49FT	1983	Ex Lightfoot, Winsford, 1989
70	IIL6443	Bedford YNV Venturer	Caetano Algarve	C53F	1988	Ex Paul Diaper, Newport, 1991
71	SIB6740	Mercedes-Benz 0303/15R	Mercedes-Benz	C49FT	1985	Ex Paul Diaper, Newport, 1991
73	D889MWR	Freight Rover Sherpa	Dormobile	B20F	1987	Ex Yorkshire Rider, 1991
79	WXI5863	DAF SB2305DHS585	Van Hool Alizée	C49FT	1988	Ex Peter Carol, Bristol, 1993
80	IIL3481	Volvo B10M-61	Jonckheere Jubilee P599	C49FT	1988	Ex Daisy Bus Services, Brigg, 1994
81	YIA972	Volvo B58-61	Duple Dominant IV	C57F	1982	Ex Arvonia, Llanrug, 1994
82	LIL3934	Volvo B10M-61	Jonckheere Jubilee P599	C49FT	1988	Ex Victory Tours, Handley, 1995

Previous Registrations:

IIL7331	D512WNV	SIB6740	C722RJU, DIA4800	NIB3214	A373UNH, RBO284, A832GEJ
IIB9140	DDG260T	KIB1767	A383ROU, JEP417	WXI5863	E629KCX
IIL3481	E33MKV, HS8882, E796NHP	LIL3934	E35MVC, HIL8127	YIA972	FHS764X
IIL6443	E762JAY				

Livery: Blue and white; pink and blue (Kingfisher Travel) 56, 67/8, 70/1, 80-2; silver (Kingfisher Travel)

Despite the changes in local government structure in Wales from April 1996, in which the Borough of Islwyn disappeared, the stand-alone nature of the transport undertaking ensured that it continued as Islwyn Borough Transport Ltd with new owners, the County Borough of Caerphilly. The fleet name style has been IBT for some time, with coaches carrying Kingfisher names. Now part of the 'old guard' of Leopards with either Marshall or Willowbrook bodies is *(top)* 14, YDW565T, a Marshall example approaching Blackwood bus station, while *(bottom)* 09, H907XGA, represents the 'new blood'. This full coach-specification Mercedes-Benz has joined the *Kingfisher* fleet. *John Jones*

JOHN'S TRAVEL

D J Davies, 19 Six Bells Estate, Heolgerrig, Merthyr Tydfil   CF48 1TU

Depot :Winchfawr, Heolgerrig and Unit B, Abercanaid Ind Est.

RGE900W	Ford R1014	Plaxton Supreme IV	C45F	1980	Ex Frenchay NHS Trust, 1993
D739JUB	Freight Rover Sherpa	Carlyle	B16F	1986	Ex Yorkshire Rider, 1989
D244VNL	Renault-Dodge S56	Alexander AM	DP19F	1987	Ex Red & White, 1994
E267BRG	Renault-Dodge S56	Alexander AM	DP19F	1987	Ex Red & White, 1994
E272BRG	Renault-Dodge S56	Alexander AM	DP19F	1987	Ex Red & White, 1994
E126AAL	Ford Transit VE6	Mellor	B16FL	1988	Ex Nottinghamshire CC, 1996
F544JRO	Ford Transit VE6	Ford	M8	1989	Ex private owner, 1992
F338XOV	Ford Transit VE6	Ford	M8	1989	Ex private owner, 1992

Livery: Blue and white

John's Travel has established a niche in the Merthyr area and continues to operate their frequent town service with little difficulty. Indeed, the arrival of former-Red & White, Renault-Dodge minibuses in 1994 rather indicated their presence was no threat to the Stagecoach subsidiary while providing a valuable public service. The only full size vehicle operated in this 10-metre Ford, RGE900W.
John Jones

JONES of BRYNCETHIN

Gwyn Jones & Son Ltd, Whitecroft Garage, Bryncethin, Bridgend CF32 9YR

JVS929N	Leyland Leopard PSU3B/4R	Duple Dominant	C53F	1975	Ex Jevis Bros, Margam, 1995
XRW511S	Leyland Leopard PSU5C/4R	Plaxton Supreme III	C57F	1978	Ex Shirley, Enderby, 1992
YFB5V	Bedford YMT	Plaxton Supreme IV	C53F	1979	
YFB6V	Bedford YMT	Plaxton Supreme IV	C53F	1979	
KYL828X	Leyland Leopard PSU5C/4R	Duple Dominant IV	C57F	1981	Ex Grey Green, 1988
SHE533Y	Leyland Tiger TRCTL11/3R	Plaxton Supreme V	C57F	1982	Ex Geoff Willetts, Pillowell, 1991
OJI9472	Leyland Tiger TRCTL11/3R	Plaxton Paramount 3500	C49FT	1984	
OJI9474	Mercedes-Benz O303/15R	Jonckheere Jubilee P50	C38FT	1984	Ex Limebourne, Battersea, 1991
VOO235	Volvo B10M-61	Van Hool Alizée	C49FT	1984	Ex Four Seasons Travel, Durham, 1993
GIJ330	Volvo B10M-61	Van Hool Alizée	C49FT	1984	Ex Halcyon Kingston-upon-Hull, 1994
OJI9477	LAG G355Z	LAG Panoramic	C49FT	1987	Ex Brylaine, Boston, 1991
OJI9475	Mercedes-Benz O303/15R	Mercedes-Benz	C49FT	1987	Ex Inland Travel, Flimwell, 1992
G837GNV	Volvo B10M-60	Jonckheere Deauville P599	C51FT	1993	Ex Swanbrook, Cheltenham, 1995

Previous Registrations:

GIJ330	A450RRH, 485DKH	OJI9474	A117SNH	OJI9477	D504YPB
OJI9472	A876YWJ	OJI9475	E913EAY	VOO235	From new

Livery: White, red, orange and maroon

Jones of Bryncethin also retain the name of their founders son Gwyn Jones, on their vehicles as shown by SHE533Y a Plaxton Supreme V-bodied Leyland Tiger. The business was started by Elfed Gwyn Jones in the late 1920s but stage services passed to Western Welsh. It was after the Second World War that a number of Bedford OWBs were acquired and coach operations continued steadily throughout the intervening years. Most of these have been Bedfords in contrast to the current fleet.
John Jones

KEN HOPKINS

Tonna Luxury Coaches Ltd; Tonna Luxury Coaches '86 Ltd, Tennis View Garage,
Heol-y-glo, Tonna, Neath & Port Talbot   SA11 3NJ

No.	Reg	Chassis	Body	Seating	Year	Notes
79	EEP395V	Bedford YMT	Duple Dominant II Express	C53F	1979	
102	VNT3S	Bedford YMT	Duple Dominant II	C53F	1978	Ex Evans, Penrhyncoch, 1983
125	99KMH	Volvo B10M-61	Plaxton Paramount 3500 III	C53F	1988	
128	561AH	Volvo B10M-61	Duple Dominant IV	C53F	1983	Ex Shearings, 1988
130	AUJ706T	Bedford YMT	Duple Dominant II	C53F	1979	Ex Rees Travel, Llanelly Hill, 1988
131	KMH39	Volvo B58-56	Duple Dominant II Express	C53F	1979	Ex British Airways, 1989
132	PXI8687	Volvo B58-56	Duple Dominant II Express	C53F	1980	Ex Thomas Bros, Llangadog, 1989
136	WYM675	Volvo B58-61	Plaxton Viewmaster III	C53F	1977	Ex Hickmott, Kingsnorth, 1990
137	JXI1753	Volvo B58-61	Plaxton Supreme III	C53F	1976	Ex Premier, Paisley, 1990
138	DHE696V	Bedford YMT	Plaxton Supreme IV	C53F	1980	Ex Maybury, Cranborne, 1991
140	HVD588N	Bedford YRT	Plaxton Elite III	C53F	1975	Ex Athelstan, Chippenham, 1991
141	FWF358V	Bedford YMT	Plaxton Supreme IV	C53F	1980	Ex Howden Mini Coaches, 1992
142	XXI7360	Volvo B58-61	Duple Dominant II	C53F	1980	Ex McCulloch, Stoneykirk, 1992
143	WXI9255	Volvo B58-61	Plaxton Elite III	C55F	1975	Ex Scorpio Travel, Gosport, 1992
144	JEC592T	Bedford YMT	Plaxton Supreme IV	C53F	1979	Ex Dudley Coachways, 1992
146	REA946W	Bedford YMT	Plaxton Supreme IV	C53F	1980	Ex Brighton, 1992
147	IIL6541	Volvo B10M-61	Plaxton Viewmaster IV	C53F	1981	Ex Dereham Coachways, 1993
148	C450WFO	Bedford CF	Dormobile	M12	1985	Ex Tristram, Resolven, 1993
150	CNR77T	Bedford YMT	Plaxton Supreme IV	C53F	1979	Ex Bob-I-Bus, Derby, 1994
151	EPC916V	Bedford YLQ	Duple Dominant II	C45F	1979	Ex Rodger, Corby, 1994
152	WSU472	Volvo B10M-61	Plaxton Viewmaster IV	C51F	1982	Ex Leisure Travel, Dover, 1994
153	93FYB	DAF MB200DKTL600	Plaxton Viewmaster IV	C53F	1982	Ex Ayres, Dalkeith, 1994
154	LAK306W	DAF MB200DKTL550	Plaxton Supreme IV	C53F	1981	Ex Jones, Birmingham, 1994
155	JIL7652	Volvo B10M-56	Plaxton Supreme VI Express	C53F	1982	Ex DRM, Bromyard, 1995
156	B208TBU	Mercedes-Benz L608D	Mellor	C19F	1985	Ex Parkin, Rainworth, 1995

Previous Registrations:

93FYB	WUT121X, 791VT	KMH39	NGR352T
99KMH	E750HJF	PXI8687	CBX828V
561AH	ENF559Y	WSU472	YBW472X
EEP395V	ATH817V, 99KMH	WXI9255	HYS53N
IIL6541	ORR425W	WYM675	TGD976R
JIL7652	KWP111X, MOI3565, MUY182X	XXI7360	WSW150V
JXI1753	NGB14P		

Livery: Two-tone grey and red

Ken Hopkins has now gathered four Plaxton Viewmasters such as IIL6541 in to his fleet which, for many years, was dominated by Duple-bodied Bedfords. The business started around 1952 with a Davies-bodied Dennis Lancet and, aside from a few Bristol LS/MW saloons, most other vehicles were indeed of the Bedford marque.
John Jones

LEN HOPKINS COACHES

Broadwest Ltd, Enfield Garage, Ogmore Vale, Bridgend   CF32 7EH

FBO305L	Leyland Leopard PSU3B/4R	Plaxton Supreme III	C44F	1973	Ex Hopkins, Ogmore Vale, 1990
ROD662N	Volvo B58-56	Duple Dominant	C53F	1975	Ex Hopkins, Ogmore Vale, 1990
JBO461N	Volvo B58-56	Plaxton Supreme III Express	C53F	1975	Ex Porthcawl, Omnibus, 1994
KBO601P	Volvo B58-56	Plaxton Supreme III Express	C49F	1975	Ex Hopkins, Ogmore Vale, 1990
UUP460R	AEC Reliance 6U3ZR	Plaxton Supreme III	C53F	1977	Ex Street, Bickington, 1996
NSU638V	Volvo B58-61	Plaxton Supreme IV	C57F	1980	Ex Lewis, Llanrhystyd, 1992
PAA826	Volvo B10M-61	Plaxton Paramount 3500	C49FT	1984	Ex Clevedon Motorways, 1992
8845EL	Volvo B10M-61	Plaxton Paramount 3500	C51F	1984	Ex Taunton Coaches, 1993
MIL3293	Volvo B10M-61	Plaxton Paramount 3500	C49FT	1985	Ex Rover Coaches, Horsley, 1995
C336UFP	DAF SB2300DHS585	Plaxton Paramount 3200 II	C53F	1986	Ex Angel Motors, Tottenham, 1995
MIL3292	Volvo B10M-61	Plaxton Paramount 3500 II	C51FT	1987	Ex Austin, Earlston, 1992

Previous Registrations:

8845EL	A702OWY, XLF622, A102VYC	MIL3293	B334SEA, KIW8610, 904DRH, B390SFH
FBO305L	MRO190L, 8845EL	PAA826	From new
MIL3292	D450CSH, LS8411, D100GSG		

Livery: White, red and silver

Len Hopkins of Ogmore Vale started with a minibus in 1959 moving onto larger coaches in 1970. The purchase of a new DAF/Plaxton Paramount in 1984 introduced a new white, silver, red and black livery, as it retained that in which it was displayed at a trade show. Mr Hopkins retired in 1990 selling the business to some former employees of Morris Travel, Pencoed. Some elements of the livery are retained on vehicles in a regularly changing line-up. Acquired just over a year ago, C336UFP is a rear-engined DAF. *Robert Edworthy*

LLYNFI COACHES

D H & M Stolzenberg, Birchgrove, Queen Marys Lane, Maesteg,
Bridgend, CF34 9SF

Depots : Coronation Road, Croeserw; Queen Marys Lane, Maesteg and Heol Ty Gwyn Ind Est, Tyle Teg, Maesteg.

FXI8505	Bedford YMT	Plaxton Supreme III	C53F	1977	Ex Galloway, Mendlesham, 1993
RPE457R	Bedford YMT	Plaxton Supreme III	C53F	1977	Ex Galloway, Mendlesham, 1993
RPV673R	Bedford YMT	Plaxton Supreme III Express	C53F	1977	Ex Galloway, Mendlesham, 1993
SHP693R	Bedford YMT	Plaxton Supreme III	C53F	1977	Ex Galloway, Mendlesham, 1993
GOI5120	Bedford YMT	Plaxton Supreme III	C53F	1977	Ex Galloway, Mendlesham, 1993
GBD888T	Bedford YMT	Plaxton Supreme IV	C53F	1979	Ex Ken Hopkins, Tonna, 1995
GBO241W	Bedford YMT	Plaxton Supreme IV	C53F	1980	Ex Ken Hopkins, Tonna, 1995
D65OKG	Freight Rover Sherpa	Carlyle	B18F	1987	Ex Hope Baptist Church, 1994
E823WWF	Mercedes-Benz 609D	Whittaker Europa	C23F	1988	Ex Whyte's Coaches, Newmachar, 1995
F511CKU	Mercedes-Benz 811D	Whittaker Europa	C23F	1988	
H366NCY	Ford Transit VE6	Ford	M14	1990	Ex Days Hire, Swansea, 1993
H974PCY	Ford Transit VE6	Ford	M8L	1990	Ex Days Hire, Swansea, 1995
H390GAV	Ford Transit VE6	Pearl	M14	1990	Ex Bown Self-drive, Caerphilly, 1992
H920WMW	Ford Transit VE6	Ford	M14	1990	Ex private owner, 1995
J145UCY	Ford Transit VE6	Ford	M14	1991	Ex Days Hire, Swansea, 1993
L839FTX	Mercedes-Benz 711D	Plaxton Beaver	DP25F	1994	

Previous Registrations:

FXI8505	OHT864R, 5611PP	GOI5120	YUE595S

Livery: White and blue

Llynfi Coaches have flitted in and out of stage carriage operation over the past few years but currently are not operating services although David Stolzenberg will not rule out re-commencement at short notice. A new garage is due to open in the summer of 1996 to replace two older premises. As a result several newer Dennis Javelins have been disposed of but should be replaced next year. L839FTX, the newest vehicle in the fleet, is seen in Bridgend while on service in 1995.
John Jones

59

MANSEL DAVID

M David, 190 Oxford Street, Pontycymmer, Bridgend CF32 8DG

RPR751K	AEC Reliance 6U3ZR	Plaxton Elite III	C57F	1972	Ex Waterhall Coaches, Kenfig Hill, 1995
SKG895S	Bristol VRT/SL3/501	Eastern Coach Works	H43/31F	1977	Ex Morris Travel, Pencoed, 1995
XBO117T	Bristol VRT/SL3/501	Eastern Coach Works	H43/31F	1979	Ex Morris Travel, Pencoed, 1995
APM116T	AEC Reliance 6U2R	Plaxton Supreme IV Express	C49F	1979	Ex Hague, Sheffield, 1996
WEB409T	AEC Reliance 6U3ZR	Plaxton Supreme IV Express	C49F	1979	Ex Cambridge Coach Services, 1993
XLB821	AEC Reliance 6U2R	Plaxton Supreme IV Express	C49F	1980	Ex Lincoln, 1991
JBZ6926	AEC Reliance 6U3ZR	Plaxton Supreme IV	C57F	1980	Ex Henley's, Abertillery, 1995

Previous Registrations:

JBZ6926	BBT380V, OAT206V	XLB821	EPM148V

Livery: various

Mansel David has favoured AEC Reliance coaches for many years and continues to acquire examples of this reliable marque. WEB409T originated with Premier Travel and, in common with most arrivals, retains its previous operators livery. Mansel David commenced operations in 1949 and acquired the businesses of Carpenter, Blaengarw in 1960, Kenfig Motors Ltd in 1977 and that of Edwards, Llangeinor in 1978. Since then, however, a steady decline in available colliery contracts amongst others has reduced fleet strength to its present size. *Byron Gage*

MARTIN

W R & A J Martin & G R Whitcombe (A H Martin & Sons), Cross Ash Garage,
Cross Ash, Abergavenny, Monmouthshire NP7 8PL

Depot : Cross Ash Garage, Cross Ash and Station Road, Ross on Wye

GCJ420N	Bedford YRQ	Plaxton Elite III Express	C45F	1974	Ex Yeoman's, Hereford, 1986
GRY626N	Bedford YRT	Plaxton Elite III Express	C53F	1975	Ex Leicester, 1984
YDD133S	Bedford YLQ	Plaxton Supreme III	C45F	1978	Ex Aztec, Bristol, 1994
XWS541V	Bedford YLQ	Plaxton Supreme IV Express	C45F	1979	Ex Sargent, Cardiff, 1990
VBM948W	Bedford YNT	Duple Dominant II	C53F	1980	Ex Palmer, Dunstable, 1987
ECJ964W	Bedford YNT	Duple Dominant II	C53F	1981	Ex Yeoman's, Tyberton, 1987
NWG990X	Bedford YNT	Plaxton Supreme VI	C53F	1982	Ex Angel Motors, Heathrow, 1990
C406WCJ	Bedford CF	Dormobile	M12	1985	Ex Humphreys, Rhayader, 1990
C488JCY	Bedford CF	Dormobile	M12	1986	Ex Briton Ferry Minibus, 1988
D568EWS	Freight Rover Sherpa	Dormobile	B16F	1986	Ex Badgerline, 1989
F898LCJ	Freight Rover Sherpa	Freight Rover	M16	1989	

Previous Registrations:
YDD133S   YDD133S, PWV693

Livery: Cream and green

Martins fleet has changed little over the past two years, indeed over the past six few additions have
been made.   A significant proportion of work, including stage service, remains centred on
Ross-on-Wye over the English border and three or four vehicles are normally kept there.   This
Bedford YNT with Plaxton Supreme VI bodywork is the newest coach in the fleet. *Robert Edworthy*

MERLYN'S

Merlyn's Coaches (Skewen) Ltd, The Lodge, 56 Siding Terrace, Skewen,
Neath & Port Talbot SA10 6RD.

KVD442P	Leyland Leopard PSU3C/4R	Plaxton Supreme III	C53F	1975	Ex Egginton, Great Wyrely, 1992
YWN721	Leyland Leopard PSU3C/4R	Plaxton Supreme III	C53F	1976	Ex Denroy Coaches, Sowerby Bridge, 1986
ATH352V	Ford R1114	Plaxton Supreme IV	C53F	1979	
WJX478V	Leyland Leopard PSU3E/4R	Plaxton Supreme IV	C53F	1980	Ex Supreme, Hadleigh, 1990
SFD254W	Leyland Leopard PSU3E/4R	Plaxton Supreme IV	C53F	1980	Ex Supreme, Hadleigh, 1990
JUH228W	Leyland Leopard PSU4F/2R	Duple Dominant	B47F	1981	Ex Merthyr Tydfil, 1989
RWN727Y	Leyland Tiger TRCTL11/2R	Plaxton Supreme V	C53F	1983	
TJI5404	Van Hool T815H	Van Hool Alizée	C49FT	1988	
TJI5405	Volvo B10M-61	Van Hool Alizée	C53F	1988	Ex Time Travel, Thornton Heath, 1995
IIL8586	Volvo B10M-61	Van Hool Alizée	C49FT	1988	Ex Main Line, Tonyrefail, 1996
J378MBX	Renault Master T35D	Cymric	M14	1991	
J379MBX	Renault Master T35D	Cymric	M14	1991	
J40MCL	Van Hool T815H	Van Hool Acron	C49FT	1992	
J469NJU	Toyota Coaster HDB30R	Caetano Optimo II	C21F	1992	

Previous Registrations:

IIL8586	E77EVL,UVE288, E889HFW	TJI4505	E315OPR
TJI5404	E291UTH	YWN721	OYU569R

Livery: White, turquoise, red and yellow

There have been no changes to the service pattern provided by Merlyns on its single route in Neath as the former Merthyr Leopard continues to operate it. For a change we switch attention to the coach fleet which has attracted a number of Van Hool products over the past few years. A recent addition is this Volvo-based Alizée, TJI5405, which was photographed displaying a Neath RFC supporters board on the occasion of a Welsh RFU cup match in 1996. *Byron Gage*

MORRIS TRAVEL

Morris Travel Ltd, Wellhouse Garage, Penprysg Road, Pencoed,
Bridgend   CF35 6LT

Depots : Penprysg Road, Pencoed and Litchard Ind Est, Bridgend.

	BUH238V	Bristol VRT/SL3/501	Eastern Coach Works	H43/31F	1980	Ex Rhondda, 1992
w	ODJ598W	Ford R1114	Duple Dominant II	C53F	1981	Ex Capitol Coaches, Cwmbran, 1994
	ODJ605W	Ford R1114	Duple Dominant II	C53F	1981	Ex Capitol Coaches, Cwmbran, 1993
	WPD29Y	Leyland Leopard PSU3G/4R	Eastern Coach Works B51	C49F	1982	Ex Berks Bucks, 1991
	PSN916Y	Leyland Tiger TRCTL11/3R	Duple Goldliner III	C46FT	1982	Ex Strathtay Scottish, 1991
	ONV651Y	Volvo B10M-61	Jonckheere Jubilee P50	C49FT	1983	Ex Wilson, Carnwath, 1993
	TXI2425	DAF MB200DKFL600	Jonckheere Jubilee P50	C51FT	1983	Ex Pan Atlas, Acton, 1989
	HIL7540	DAF MB230DKFL615	Duple 340	C55F	1987	
	HIL7542	DAF SB2305DHS615	Duple 340	C51FT	1987	Ex Capitol Coaches, Cwmbran, 1990
	LIL7332	DAF SB2305DHS585	Jonckheere Deauville P599	C49FT	1988	Ex Gray Line, Bicester, 1996
	H122YGG	Ford Transit VE6	Deansgate	M14	1990	Ex Mansel David, Pontycymmer, 1995

Previous Registrations:

HIL7540	D27MTG	PSN916Y	SSJ135Y, WLT943	LIL7332	E670WKW, SPV860, E750DJO
HIL7542	D55NHB	TXI2425	NNV610Y		

Livery: White, blue and yellow

Morris Travel have been established at Pencoed since the Second World War after which expansion was quite rapid. Double decks have featured intermittently from the first four Birmingham Corporation Daimler COG5 in 1949 via six former BMMO D9 and a similar number of Glasgow Atlanteans in the mid 1970s. From then until now there has been a continued presence. Only one such vehicle remains in the mid 1990s however. The coach fleet has been DAF-based for several years and HIL7542 illustrates this. *Byron Gage*

NELSON'S TRAVEL

Nelson & Son (Glyn Neath) Ltd, Lamb & Flag, Glyn Neath, Neath & Port Talbot SA11 5EP

Depot : White Hart Garage, Glyn Neath

RJI2724	Leyland Leopard PSU4B/4R	Plaxton Elite III	C41F	1972	Ex Bluebird of Weymouth, 1993
PUJ998M	Ford R1114	Duple Dominant	C53F	1974	Ex Morris, Bridgnorth, 1977
WFX481	Leyland Leopard PSU5C/4R	Plaxton Supreme III	C57F	1978	Ex Geoff Willetts, Pillowell, 1993
AYR323T	Leyland National 10351A/2R		DP44F	1979	Ex London Buses, 1991
CFX318T	Ford R1014	Plaxton Supreme IV	C41F	1979	Ex Excelsior, Bournemouth, 1983
UJI1765	Mercedes Benz L608D	Plaxton Mini Supreme	C25F	1984	Ex M&J Travel, Newcastle (Shrops), 1996
LVS419V	Leyland Leopard PSU5C/4R	Duple Dominant II	C57F	1980	Ex Geoff Willetts, Pillowell, 1996
PJI3546	DAF MB200DKFL600	LAG Galaxy	C53F	1985	
PJI3549	Bedford YNV Venturer	Caetano Algarve	C53F	1988	
PJI3547	DAF SB2305DHS585	Van Hool Alizée	C55F	1988	Ex Armchair, Brentford, 1995
PJI3548	DAF MB230LT615	Van Hool Alizée	C51FT	1988	Ex Robinson's, Great Harwood, 1994
PJI3550	DAF SB2305DHTD585	Plaxton Paramount 3200 III	C53F	1989	Ex Smith's Alcester, 1990

Previous Registrations:

PJI3546	C793RJU	PJI3549	E756JAY	UJI1765	A425VDS
PJI3547	E605LVH	PJI3550	F266RJX	WFX481	XNM818S
PJI3548	E220KFV	RJI2724	HHA179L		

Livery: Cream, red and black

Nelson's smart, small fleet is based at Glyn Neath which lies towards the head of the Vale of Neath. This area is still heavily involved in coal mining, mostly open-cast, although South Wales sole remaining deep mine at Tower Colliery is some eight kilometres to the east. The only service bus operated is AYR323T, a former London Buses Leyland National which has been converted to single-door layout. It is employed mostly on schools contracts and is seen here at Pontneddfechan returning, across the county boundary, to Glyn Neath. *John Jones*

NEWPORT TRANSPORT

Newport Transport Ltd, 160 Corporation Road, Newport   NP9 0WF

| 1 | J905UBO | Leyland Tiger TRCL10/3ARZA | Plaxton Paramount 3200 III | C53F | 1991 | |
| 2 | J96NJT | Scania K113CRB | Plaxton Premiére 350 | C49FT | 1992 | Ex Excelsior, Bournemouth, 1996 |

4-9   Scania N113CRB   Alexander Strider   B48F   1993

| 4 | K104YTX | 6 | K106YTX | 7 | K107YTX | 8 | K108YTX | 9 | K109YTX |
| 5 | K105YTX | | | | | | | | |

10-18   Scania BR112DH   Wadham Stringer Vanguard   B42F   1983

| 10 | RUH10Y | 12 | RUH12Y | 14 | RUH14Y | 16 | RUH16Y | 18 | RUH18Y |
| 11 | RUH11Y | 13 | RUH13Y | 15 | RUH15Y | 17 | RUH17Y | | |

19-26   Scania N112DH   Alexander RH   H47/31F   1984

| 19 | B219YUH | 21 | B221YUH | 23 | B223YUH | 25 | B225YUH | 26 | B226YUH |
| 20 | B220YUH | 22 | B222YUH | 24 | B224YUH | | | | |

27-34   Scania N112DRB   East Lancashire   H43/33F   1986

| 27 | C27ETG | 29 | C29ETG | 31 | C31ETG | 33 | C33ETG | 34 | C34ETG |
| 28 | C28ETG | 30 | C30ETG | 32 | C32ETG | | | | |

37	E37UBO	MCW MetroRider MF150	MCW	DP25F	1988	
38	E38UBO	MCW MetroRider MF150	MCW	DP25F	1988	
39	D478PON	MCW MetroRider MF150/14	MCW	B23F	1987	Ex Parfitt's, Rhymney Bridge, 1994
40	XFM203	Leyland Tiger TRCTL11/3RH	Duple 340	C49FT	1986	Ex Crosville, 1988

41-52   Scania N113DRB   Alexander RH   H47/31F   1988-89

41	F41YHB	44	F44YHB	47	G47FKG	49	G49FKG	51	G51FKG
42	F42YHB	45	F45YHB	48	G48FKG	50	G50FKG	52	G52FKG
43	F43YHB	46	F46YHB						

53-58   Optare MetroRider MR09   Optare   B23F   1990

| 53 | G53KTX | 55 | G55KTX | 56 | G56KTX | 57 | G57KTX | 58 | G58KTX |
| 54 | G54KTX | | | | | | | | |

59-64   Optare MetroRider   Optare   B23F   1991

| 59 | H59PNY | 61 | H61PNY | 62 | H62PNY | 63 | H63PNY | 64 | H64PNY |
| 60 | H160PNY | | | | | | | | |

The first Scania N-series buses for the United Kingdom market comprised a batch of eight for Newport in December 1984. They remained the only examples until the 1986 delivery of a further eight. The latter were bodied by East Lancashire, the original batch, including 20, B220YUH, by Alexander.
John Jones

Newports quest for standardisation has been aided by the few design changes to the Alexander R-type body since its launch. This highly successful style was launched in 1980 and the main variation in parts exist between the normal-height RH and low-height RL versions. All of Newport's Alexander double-decks are RH versions including 46, F46YHB, *John Jones*

65	M65KTG	Scania N113CRL	Alexander Strider	B48F	1995
66	M166KTG	Scania N113CRL	Alexander Strider	B48F	1995
67	M67KTG	Scania N113CRL	Alexander Strider	B48F	1995

68-73

		Scania N113CRB		Alexander Strider		B48F		1994		
68	L68EKG	70	L170EKG	71	L71EKG	72	L172EKG	73	L73EKG
69	L69EKG								

74-83

		Scania N113CRL		Alexander Strider		B48F		1995-96		
74	M74KTG	76	M76KTG	79	N79PDW	81	N81PDW	83	N83PDW
75	M75KTG	78	N78PDW	80	N180PDW	82	N82PDW		

93-100

		Scania BR112DH		Marshall		H45/31F		1982-83		
93	PTG93Y	96	PTG96Y	98	PTG98Y	99	PTG99Y	100	PTG100Y
95	PTG95Y	97	PTG97Y						

| 102 | YDW758K | Metro-Scania BR111MH | MCW | B40D | 1972 |
| 178 | PDW484 | Leyland Titan PD2/40 | Longwell Green | H30/28R | 1958 |

Previous Registrations:

| J96NJT | A15XEL | | XFM203 | C73KLG |

Livery: Green and cream; cream and green (coaches 1/2, 40)

Opposite top: Newport Transport 39, D478PON, was acquired in 1994 for use on a service between the bus station and the town's Royal Gwent Hospital and it is seen operating this service in May 1996. This former London Buses MCW MetroRider was acquired via Parfitt's, Rhymney Bridge. *John Jones*

Opposite bottom: Following a move away from double deckers, Newport Transport has steadily been replacing them with new saloons. Delivered earlier this year, 79, N79PDW represents the fourth consecutive batch of Alexander Strider bodied Scania N113's. They are noteworthy in being the first buses for many years to bear the original Newport 'DW' index marks. *John Jones*

PERRY'S SUPREME

K, ME, BR & PR Perry, 4 New Road, Woodfieldside, Blackwood, Caerphilly NP2 0BU

YVC20L	Bedford VAL70	Plaxton Elite II	C53F	1972	Ex Price, Halesowen, 1975
NNY817L	Bedford YRT	Plaxton Elite III	C53F	1973	Ex Davies, Pen-y-graig, 1981
PNK154R	Bedford YMT	Van Hool McArdle	C53F	1977	Ex Monk, Staplecross, 1983
PHB901R	Bedford YLQ	Plaxton Supreme III	C45F	1977	Ex Ambassador Cs, Bargoed, 1996
LTA879W	Bedford YMT	Duple Dominant II	C53F	1980	Ex Rees Travel, Llanelly Hill, 1997
NAY429W	Ford R1114	Caetano Alpha	C53F	1980	Ex Hoskin, Blackwood, 1988
A298SPS	Bedford VAS5	Plaxton Supreme IV	C25FL	1983	Ex Shetland Islands Council, 1992
B371PLK	Mercedes-Benz L310	Devon Conversions	M12	1985	Ex Budget Rental, Heathrow, 1992
D600KTX	Ford Transit	Ford	M14	1987	Ex private owner, 1994
E717MFS	Freight Rover Sherpa	Freight Rover	M16	1988	Ex Howells, Deri, 1988
J404NBA	Leyland-DAF 400	Made-to-Measure	M16	1992	Ex private owner, 1996

Livery: Cream and orange

It is an oft-quoted truism that 'there are not many Bedford VALs in use today'. It helps if you come across one of the last to be built such as Perrys YVC20L. New to Harry Shaw this Plaxton Panorama Elite II bodied VAL70 was among the last two-dozen licensed. It is retained in immaculate condition for a twenty-four year old PCV in daily use and was photographed approaching Barry Island for the Welsh Bus Rally. *John Jones*

The South Wales Bus Handbook

PHIL ANSLOW TRAVEL

P Anslow/S J Anslow/Gwent Omnibus Co Ltd, Unit 10, Pontnewynydd Ind Est,
Pontnewynydd, Pontypool, Torfaen   NP4 6YW

YHY586J	Bristol RELL6L	Eastern Coach Works	B50F	1971	Ex Smiths of Portland, 1996
YHY596J	Bristol RELL6L	Eastern Coach Works	B50F	1971	Ex Smiths of Portland, 1996
DAE511K	Bristol RELL6L	Eastern Coach Works	B50F	1972	Ex Badgerline, 1993
HHW915L	Bristol RELL6L	Eastern Coach Works	B50F	1972	Ex Badgerline, 1993
HHW917L	Bristol RELL6L	Eastern Coach Works	B50F	1972	Ex Gary's, Tredegar, 1994
LHT170L	Bristol RELL6L	Eastern Coach Works	B50F	1973	Ex Badgerline, 1994
LHT173L	Bristol RELL6L	Eastern Coach Works	B50F	1971	Ex Smiths of Portland, 1996
OAE954M	Bristol RELL6L	Eastern Coach Works	B50F	1973	Ex Badgerline, 1993
DAD258T	Leyland Leopard PSU3E/4R	Plaxton Supreme IV	C57F	1979	Ex IBT, 1995
IIB9140	Leyland Leopard PSU5C/4R	Plaxton Supreme IV	C57F	1979	Ex IBT, 1995
BVA784V	Leyland Leopard PSU3F/4R	Plaxton Supreme IV Express	C49F	1980	Ex Premier Travel, 1991
DNP444W	Volvo B58-56	Plaxton Supreme IV Express	C53F	1981	Ex Empress Motors, Bethnal Green, 1994
A539XUH	Bedford VAS5	Plaxton Supreme IV	C29FL	1984	Ex Gwent CC, 1996
HIL8285	Leyland Tiger TRCTL11/3RZ	Duple 340	C53F	1986	Ex Mid Wales Motorways, 1995
D182LAX	Bedford YMP	Plaxton Paramount 3200 II	C31F	1986	Ex Capitol, New Inn, 1996

	Iveco Daily 49.10	Robin Hood City Nippy	B19F	1987	Ex City Line, 1994-95
D911HOU	D913HOU	D918HOU		D919HOU	D920HOU
D912HOU	D917HOU				

TJI4123	Volvo B10M-61	Plaxton Paramount 3200 II	C48FT	1987	Ex Express Travel, 1994
TJI4124	Volvo B10M-61	Plaxton Paramount 3200 II	C48FT	1987	Ex Express Travel, 1994

There has been an extensive transformation in the Phil Anslow Travel fleet since its appearance in the previous edition of this Bus Handbook. All of the Freight Rover Sherpas were swept away through the acquisition of two batches of Iveco Dailys from City Line at Bristol. First to arrive were eleven E-registered 21-seaters including E958LAE seen at Pontypool. Later arrivals were seven D-registered, 19 seaters. Many will be replaced by new vehicles delivered over the next fifteen months. *John Jones*

Provision of a Sainsburys Superstore contract in 1995 prompted the purchase of Phil Anslows first new coach, a Caetano Optimo-bodied Toyota. This handy-sized vehicle provides full coach standard comfort in a compact vehicle and enhances the image of coach travel for smaller parties. *John Jones*

	Iveco Daily 49.10	Robin Hood City Nippy	B21F	1987	Ex City Line, 1994	
E947LAE	E949LAE	E953LAE		E955LAE		E957LAE
E948LAE	E950LAE	E954LAE		E956LAE		E958LAE
F230DGB	Dennis Javelin 12SDA1907	Duple 320	C53FT	1988	Ex C&E Travel, Blaenavon, 1996	
F232OFP	Dennis Javelin 12SDA1907	Duple 320	C53FT	1988	Ex Owen, Oswestry, 1993	
F58YBO	Leyland Tiger TRCTL11/3ARZ	Duple 320	C53F	1989	Ex Thornes, Bubwith, 1995	
G797RNC	Leyland Tiger TRCTL11/3RZ	Duple 320	C53F	1989	Ex Shearings, 1994	
G798RNC	Leyland Tiger TRCTL11/3RZ	Duple 320	C53F	1989	Ex Shearings, 1994	
	Mercedes-Benz 709D	Dormobile Routemaker	B29F	1993		
K205OHS	L913UGA	L927UGA		L928UGA		L929UGA
K206OHS	L914UGA					
L936KSG	Iveco Turbodaily 59.12	Dormobile Routemaker	B25F	1993	Ex Rennies, Dunfermline, 1994	
L937KSG	Iveco Turbodaily 59.12	Dormobile Routemaker	B29F	1993	Ex Rennies, Dunfermline, 1994	
L355YNR	Dennis Javelin 12SDA2131	Plaxton Premiére 320	C53F	1993	Ex Irvine, Law, 1995	
M91JHB	Mercedes-Benz 709D	WS Wessex II	B29F	1995		
M92JHB	Mercedes-Benz 709D	WS Wessex II	B29F	1995		
M93JHB	Mercedes-Benz 811D	WS Wessex II	B33F	1995		
N112OBO	Toyota Coaster HZB50R	Caetano Optimo III	C21F	1995		
N417UWN	Iveco TurboDaily 59.12	UVG Citi Star	DP29F	1996		
N418UWN	Iveco TurboDaily 59.12	UVG Citi Star	DP29F	1996		
N419UWN	Iveco TurboDaily 59.12	UVG Citi Star	DP29F	1996		

Previous Registrations:

HIL8285	C213NFV		TJI4123	D444CNR, NXI900?, D996UKA
IIB9140	DDG260T		TJI4124	D445CNR, NXI900?, D998UKA

Livery: Green, yellow, and white (buses); white, red and blue (coaches)

Opposite, top: Phil Anslow Travel has the distinction of operating one of the largest remaining fleets of Bristol REs. All of them were formerly operated by Badgerline and four, including the one illustrated, were acquired direct. OAE954M is seen at Varteg Hill on a school contract. *John Jones*

After a period of dual-sourcing its new bus requirements from Mercedes-Benz and Iveco, Phil Anslow Travel has established a preference for the latter, with three Turbo Daily 59.12s delivered earlier this year and more on order. N419UWN, with UVG Citi Star bodywork is seen in Pontypool. *John Jones*

The South Wales Bus Handbook

PHILLIPS

Phillips Coaches Ltd, 1 Rheola Street, Penrhiwceiber, Mountain Ash,
Rhondda Cynon Taff   CF45 3TA

Depot : Main Road, Pentwyn Bridge, Penrhiwceiber

GNY433C	Leyland Titan PD3/4	Massey	L35/33RD	1965	Ex Rhymney Valley, 1981
TDW312J	Leyland Atlantean PDR1A/1	Alexander J	H43/31F	1971	Ex Stan Bowers, Bridgend, 1985
NRG164M	Leyland Atlantean AN68/1R	Alexander AL	H45/36F	1973	Ex Lonsdale Coaches, Heysham, 1992
NRG169M	Leyland Atlantean AN68/1R	Alexander AL	H45/36F	1973	Ex Lonsdale Coaches, Heysham, 1991
VBA176S	Leyland Atlantean AN68A/1R	Northern Counties	H43/32F	1978	Ex GM Buses, 1991
WWO811T	Bedford YMT	Plaxton Supreme III	C53F	1978	Ex Stan Bowers, Bridgend, 1985
JIL7903	Leyland Leopard PSU5C/4R	Plaxton Supreme IV	C53F	1979	Ex Tony's Minibus, Hasland, 1997
NPP345V	Bedford YMT	Plaxton Supreme IV	C53F	1980	Ex Lewis Coaches, Cwmaman, 1993
PBC461W	Bedford YMT	Duple Dominant IV Express	C53F	1981	
EAE684W	Ford Transit 190	Ford	M12	1981	Ex private owner, 1994
WWD106X	Ford Transit 190	Tricentrol	M12	1982	Ex Lewis Coaches, Cwmaman, 1992
VJU125X	Bedford YMT	Duple Dominant IV Express	C53F	1982	
BFP260Y	Bedford YNT	Plaxton Paramount 3200 E	C53F	1983	
DSV520	Leyland Tiger TRCTL11/3R	Plaxton Paramount 3200	C53F	1983	Ex Hodgson, Chatburn, 1987
A270HAY	Ford Transit	Yeates	M12	1984	

Previous Registrations:

DSV520	FCK449Y	JIL7903	HGN307T

Livery: Cream, orange, red and brown (coaches); maroon (buses)

While half-cab double deckers may be two-a-penny in some quarters of the country there are few genuine lowbridge specification examples, and regrettably even fewer Massey-built ones still in regular use. Phillips have kept GNY433C going since 1981 when it was already sixteen years since it entered service with Caerphilly UDC. *John Jones*

PORTHCAWL OMNIBUS Co

The Porthcawl Omnibus Co Ltd, Old Station Lane, Porthcawl,
Bridgend   CF36 5TL
J Williams, The Little Grange, 176 New Road, Porthcawl, Bridgend CF36 5BH

WTH171M	Leyland Leopard PSU3B/4RT	Plaxton Elite III Express	C53F	1973	Ex Evans, Brynamman, 1991
ROM125M	Leyland Leopard PSU3B/4R	Plaxton Elite III Express	C53F	1974	Ex Catch-a-Bus, East Boldon, 1989
PNY391R	Leyland Leopard PSU5A/4R	East Lancs EL2000 (1994)	B51F	1977	Ex Rees & Williams, 1995
UCY843S	Leyland Leopard PSU5C/4R	East Lancs EL2000 (1994)	B51F	1978	Ex Rees & Williams, 1995
DWY662T	Leyland Leopard PSU3E/4R	Plaxton Supreme IV Express	C49F	1978	Ex Brewers, 1992
GWU562T	Leyland Leopard PSU3E/4R	Plaxton Supreme IV	C49F	1979	Ex Brewers, 1991
AAL423A	Leyland Leopard PSU5D/4R	Plaxton P3200 III (1987)	C53F	1980	Ex Birmingham Coach Co, 1992
LNV795	Volvo B58-61	Jonckheere Bermuda	C51F	1980	Ex Baker, Weston-s-Mare, 1989
LWG533W	Leyland Leopard PSU3E/4R	Plaxton Supreme IV	C49F	1981	Ex Reed's Travel, Kinsley, 1992
LWN790X	Bedford YNT	Duple Dominant IV	C53F	1982	Ex Rees & Williams, 1986
VKN835X	Leyland Leopard PSU3F/4R	Willowbrook 003	C47F	1982	Ex Maidstone & District, 1994
VKN837X	Leyland Leopard PSU3F/4R	Willowbrook 003	C47F	1982	Ex Maidstone & District, 1994
SMY634X	Leyland Tiger TRCTL11/3R	Plaxton Supreme V	C50F	1982	Ex Graham's, Kelvedon, 1993
C349RPE	Ford Transit 190D	Carlyle	B16F	1986	Ex Alder Valley South, 1988
C350RPE	Ford Transit 190D	Carlyle	B16F	1986	Ex Alder Valley South, 1988
D820SGB	Volvo B10M-61	Plaxton Paramount 3500 III	C49FT	1987	Ex Atkinson, Ingleby Arncliffe, 1995
H335LAN	Mercedes-Benz 811D	Reeve Burgess Beaver	B33F	1991	Ex Oakley Buses, 1995

Previous Registrations:

AAL423A	BUH223V	LNV795	GPA628V	UCY843S	WFH173S, MKH824A

Livery: Maroon and beige or maroon and white

**Porthcawl Omnibus continue their small network of services in and around the seaside town
including their express, Cardiff-Porthcawl, X14 service which uses the M4 for much of its length.
One of the more regular performers on this route is AAL423A one of two National Welsh Leyland
Leopards that were rebodied in 1987 after a fire destroyed their original Plaxton bodies.** *John Jones*

PULLMAN COACHES

Pullman Coaches Ltd; CW Lewis & HS Rees, Unit 41 Penclawdd Industrial Estate, Crofty, Swansea SA4 3RS

IIB9890	Leyland Leopard PSU3E/4R	Plaxton Supreme IV	C49F	1980	Ex IBT, 1992
GAX138W	Leyland Leopard PSU4F/2R	Marshall	B45F	1981	Ex IBT, 1991
GDE383W	Ford R1114	Plaxton Supreme IV	C53F	1981	Ex Taf Valley Coaches, Whitland, 1994
A106YEP	Leyland Tiger TRCTL11/3R	Plaxton Paramount 3200	C46FT	1983	Ex Swansea Coach Company, 1994
SIB7240	Leyland Tiger TRCTL11/3R	Duple Laser	C53F	1984	Ex IBT, 1995
D407NUH	Dodge Commando GO8	East Lancashire	DP25F	1987	Ex IBT, 1994
TJI1702	Volvo B10M-61	Plaxton Paramount 3200 III	C53F	1988	Ex Primrose, Leominster, 1995
TJI4030	Volvo B10M-61	Plaxton Paramount 3500 III	C49FT	1988	Ex Warner's, Tewkesbury, 1995
TJI4700	DAF MB230LB615	Van Hool Alizée	C51FT	1990	Ex Freestone Cs, Beetley, 1995
G923LTH	Leyland-DAF 200	Leyland-DAF	M12	1990	
L2PCL	Renault Trafic	Cymric	M11L	1993	
N2PCL	Dennis Javelin 12SDA2159	Plaxton Premiére 350	C51FT	1995	
N753VCY	DAF MB230LT615	Van Hool Alizée	C49FT	1996	

Previous Registrations:

A106YEP	A101HNC, PJI3379, A101OVF, A20SCC	TJI1702	E726LWP
GDE383W	PDG100W, 3622AD, JMR394W, 3432RE	TJI4030	E325UUB
IIB9890	YHW609V	TJI4700	G970KJX
SIB7240	A221VWO, AKG134A		

Livery: Cream/white, red and fawn; white, blue and green (Leger Travel) N753VCY

Pullman have made further forays into service work with an experimental Rail-link route and another local service. Unusually these involved brand new vehicles, a rare occurrence for a small operator. Unfortunately neither ventures continue and the Mercedes-Benz minibus for the former passed to SWT. The Dennis Dart returned to its supplying dealer being replaced by a new DAF/Van Hool Coach. Last years new coach, N2PCL a Dennis Javelin with Plaxton Première 350 body is seen below. *Robert Edworthy.*

RED & WHITE

Red & White Services Ltd; The Valleys Bus Company Ltd; Aberdare Bus Company Ltd, 1 St David's Road, Cwmbran, Torfaen NP44 1QX

Depots and outstations: Red & White - Mill Street, Abergavenny; Bishops Meadow, Brecon; Warwick Road, Brynmawr; Cinderford; Bulwark Road, Chepstow; Risca Road, Crosskeys; St David's Road, Cwmbran; Lydney; Ross on Wye; **The Valleys** - Merthyr Industrial Estate, Pant, Merthyr Tydfil; Commercial Street, Pengam; **Aberdare Bus** - Cwmbach New Road, Cwmbach, Aberdare.

Part of Stagecoach plc

11w	E292TAX	Renault-Dodge S56	Northern Counties	DP25F	1988	Ex Cynon Valley, 1992
22w	G21CSG	Renault-Dodge S56	Reeve Burgess Beaver	B25F	1989	Ex Fife Scottish, 1994
25	G24CSG	Renault-Dodge S56	Reeve Burgess Beaver	B25F	1989	Ex Fife Scottish, 1994
282w	D544RCK	Mercedes-Benz L608D	Reeve Burgess	B25F	1986	Ex Ribble, 1994
283	D540RCK	Mercedes-Benz L608D	Reeve Burgess	B20F	1986	Ex Ribble, 1994
286w	C902HWF	Mercedes-Benz L608D	Reeve Burgess	B25F	1985	Ex Bluebird, 1994
301	H301PAX	Mercedes-Benz 709D	PMT Ami	C25F	1991	
302	J302TUH	Mercedes-Benz 709D	PMT Bursley	B25F	1991	
303	J303TUH	Mercedes-Benz 709D	PMT Bursley	B25F	1991	

304-317

		Mercedes-Benz 811D		Wright NimBus		B33F		1992
304	J304UKG	307	J307UKG	311	K311YKG	314	K314YKG	316	K316YKG
305	J305UKG	309	K309YKG	312	K312YKG	315	K315YKG	317	K317YKG
306	J306UKG	310	K310YKG	313	K313YKG				

318	K318YKG	Mercedes-Benz 709D	Wright NimBus	B25F	1992	
319	K319YKG	Mercedes-Benz 709D	Alexander Sprint	B25F	1992	
320	K320YKG	Mercedes-Benz 709D	Alexander Sprint	B25F	1992	
321	K321YKG	Mercedes-Benz 709D	Alexander Sprint	B25F	1992	
322	K322YKG	Mercedes-Benz 811D	Wright NimBus	B33F	1992	
323	K323YKG	Mercedes-Benz 811D	Wright NimBus	B33F	1992	
324	K324YKG	Mercedes-Benz 811D	Wright NimBus	B33F	1992	
325	K325YKG	Mercedes-Benz 811D	Wright NimBus	B33F	1992	
326	L326CHB	Mercedes-Benz 811D	Marshall C16	B33F	1993	
327	L327CHB	Mercedes-Benz 811D	Marshall C16	B33F	1993	
328	L328CHB	Mercedes-Benz 811D	Marshall C16	B33F	1993	
329	L329CHB	Mercedes-Benz 811D	Marshall C16	B33F	1993	
330	L685CDD	Mercedes-Benz 709D	Alexander Sprint	B25F	1994	Ex Cheltenham & Gloucester, 1994
331	L331CHB	Mercedes-Benz 811D	Marshall C16	B33F	1993	
332	H556TUG	Mercedes-Benz 709D	Dormobile Routemaker	DP27F	1990	Ex Graham's, Tredegar, 1994

334-360

		Mercedes-Benz 709D		Alexander Sprint		B25F		1994
334	L334FWO	340	L340FWO	346	M346JBO	351	M351JBO	356	M356JBO
335	L335FWO	341	L341FWO	347	M347JBO	352	M352JBO	357	M357JBO
336	L336FWO	342	L342FWO	348	M348JBO	353	M353JBO	358	M358JBO
337	L337FWO	343	L343FWO	349	M349JBO	354	M354JBO	359	M359JBO
338	L338FWO	344	M344JBO	350	M350JBO	355	M355JBO	360	M360JBO
339	L339FWO	345	M345JBO						

361-371

		Mercedes-Benz 709D		Alexander Sprint		B25F		1995
361	M361LAX	364	M364LAX	366	M366LAX	368	M368LAX	370	M370LAX
362	M362LAX	365	M365LAX	367	M367LAX	369	M369LAX	371	M371LAX
363	M363LAX							

Now a rapidly vanishing species with Red & White are the Mercedes-Benz L608D which, in turn, had helped to replace the large inherited fleet of Freight Rover Sherpas. Along with the remaining Renault Dodge these will soon be eliminated as further Stagecoach standard 709D/Alexander Sprint enter service. Meanwhile 283, D540RCK survives and is seen passing the brutalist architecture of Cwmbran town centre. *John Jones*

372-384

	Mercedes-Benz 709D			Alexander Sprint		B25F	1996		
372	N372PNY	375	N375PNY	378	N378PNY	381	N381PNY	383	N383PNY
373	N373PNY	376	N376PNY	379	N379PNY	382	N382PNY	384	N384PNY
374	N374PNY	377	N377PNY	380	N380PNY				

391	GHB146N	Bristol RESL6L	Eastern Coach Works	B44F	1974	Ex Cynon Valley, 1992
392	HTG354N	Bristol RESL6L	Eastern Coach Works	B44F	1975	Ex Cynon Valley, 1992
393	GHB148N	Bristol RESL6L	Eastern Coach Works	B44F	1974	Ex Cynon Valley, 1992
394	D109NDW	Leyland Lynx LX112TL11ZR1	Leyland Lynx	B48F	1987	Ex Cynon Valley, 1992
395	E113RBO	Leyland Lynx LX112TL11ZR1	Leyland Lynx	B48F	1987	Ex Cynon Valley, 1992
396	E114SDW	Leyland Lynx LX112TL11ZR1	Leyland Lynx	B48F	1987	Ex Cynon Valley, 1992
397	E115SDW	Leyland Lynx LX112TL11ZR1	Leyland Lynx	B48F	1988	Ex Cynon Valley, 1992
398	F74DCW	Leyland Lynx LX2R11C15Z4R	Leyland Lynx 2	DP45F	1989	Ex Cynon Valley, 1992
420	NWO454R	Leyland National 11351A/1R/SC		DP48F	1977	Ex National Welsh, 1991
423	NWO457R	Leyland National 11351A/1R/SC		DP48F	1977	Ex National Welsh, 1991
427	NWO461R	Leyland National 11351A/1R/SC		DP48F	1977	Ex National Welsh, 1991
434	NWO468R	Leyland National 11351A/1R/SC		DP48F	1977	Ex National Welsh, 1991
442	UTX726S	Leyland National 10351A/1R		B44F	1978	Ex Cynon Valley, 1992
448	DDW433V	Leyland National 10351A/1R		B44F	1980	Ex Cynon Valley, 1992
449	DDW434V	Leyland National 10351A/1R		B44F	1980	Ex Cynon Valley, 1992
500	YSX934W	Leyland National 2 NL106L11/1R		B44F	1981	Ex Fife Scottish, 1994
501	RSG814V	Leyland National 2 NL116L11/1R		B52F	1980	Ex Fife Scottish, 1994
502	YSX932W	Leyland National 2 NL106L11/1R		B44F	1981	Ex Fife Scottish, 1994
503	YSX933W	Leyland National 2 NL106L11/1R		B44F	1981	Ex Fife Scottish, 1994
504	MSO13W	Leyland National 2 NL116L11/1R		B52F	1980	Ex Fife Scottish, 1994
505	RSG815V	Leyland National 2 NL116L11/1R		B52F	1980	Ex Fife Scottish, 1994

Opposite, top: Red & White received eighteen Leyland National 2s from fellow Stagecoach subsidiary Fife Scottish in 1994-95. Although one has recently been transferred to Midland Red, the others remain and 505, RSG815V, is seen in Hanbury Road, Pontypool in April 1996. In NBC days, National Welsh purchased only three National 2s. *John Jones*

Opposite, bottom: Since the last edition of this book, Red & White has received twenty of the Alexander PS bodied Volvo B10M. One of these impressive machines, 753 (M753LAX) is seen in Castle Street, Merthyr Tydfil on a route which, for many years saw elderly doubledecks from of Wheatsheaf Motors.

Stagecoach has promoted the existing Red and White express routes quite strongly and has invested in new Plaxton Inter urban-bodied Dennis Javelins for the X4/X40 and X15. The X74 however remain the preserve of Leyland Tigers with Plaxton Paramount 3200 Express bodies such as 907, AAL575A arriving in Newport. *John Jones*

507	WAS767V	Leyland National 2 NL116L11/1R	B52F	1980	Ex Fife Scottish, 1994
508	MSO14W	Leyland National 2 NL116L11/1R	B52F	1980	Ex Fife Scottish, 1994
509	YSX926W	Leyland National 2 NL106L11/1R	B44F	1981	Ex Fife Scottish, 1994
510	YSX935W	Leyland National 2 NL106L11/1R	B44F	1981	Ex Fife Scottish, 1994
512	RSG824V	Leyland National 2 NL116L11/1R	B52F	1980	Ex Fife Scottish, 1994
513	RSG825V	Leyland National 2 NL116L11/1R	B52F	1980	Ex Fife Scottish, 1994
514	RSG823V	Leyland National 2 NL116L11/1R	B52F	1980	Ex Fife Scottish, 1995
515	DMS22V	Leyland National 2 NL116L11/1R	B52F	1980	Ex Fife Scottish, 1995
516	NLS987W	Leyland National 2 NL116L11/1R	B52F	1980	Ex Fife Scottish, 1995
517	DMS20V	Leyland National 2 NL116L11/1R	B52F	1980	Ex Fife Scottish, 1995

598-649

		Leyland National 11351A/1R		B49F	1977-79 Ex National Welsh, 1991

609/35/49 are fitted with Volvo engines, 619 DAF.

598	SKG908S	619	SKG923S	634	WUH167T	646	BUH211V	649	BUH214V
609	PKG741R	633	WUH166T	635	WUH168T	647	BUH212V		

651	NOE552R	Leyland National 11351A/1R	B49F	1976	Ex Cheltenham & Gloucester, 1991
652	NOE573R	Leyland National 11351A/1R(Volvo)	B49F	1976	Ex Midland Red South, 1992
653	NOE572R	Leyland National 11351A/1R(DAF)	B49F	1977	Ex Midland Red South, 1992
654	NOE576R	Leyland National 11351A/1R	B49F	1976	Ex Midland Red South, 1992
658	BPT903S	Leyland National 11351A/1R	B49F	1978	Ex Go-Ahead Northern, 1992
660	XVV540S	Leyland National 11351A/1R	B49F	1976	Ex City Line, 1993
661	MFN114R	Leyland National 11351A/1R	B49F	1976	Ex City Line, 1993
663	PHW985S	Leyland National 11351A/1R(DAF)	B52F	1978	Ex Cheltenham & Gloucester, 1995

701-708

		Volvo B6-9.9M		Alexander Dash		B40F	1994		
701	L701FWO	703	L703FWO	705	L705FWO	707	L707FWO	708	L708FWO
702	L702FWO	704	L704FWO	706	L706FWO				

If another seven or more Mercedes minibuses arrive with Red & White renumbering of the three remaining former Cynon Valley Bristol REs seems inevitable. That they have lasted so long as 'non-standard' vehicles suggests their reliability outstrips that of the series 1 Nationals, the number of which continue to drop. *Above* shows 391, GHB146N, arriving at Barry Island. Bristol VR stock has dropped to eight examples new to National Welsh while pre-owned arrivals total ten. Seen in Newbridge, 836, GTX738W, is one of the genuine home-grown versions but even this has succumbed to an engine transplant. *John Jones*

The Gloucester-Hereford service 38 is the regular haunt of the three Leyland Titans inherited from Stagecoach Selkent two years ago. Although arriving from London these vehicles were, of course, new to West Midlands PTE as part of their experimental batch. Unlike London's own extensive fleet of 1125 vehicles these, including 865, WDA1T, were single-door layout. *Robert Edworthy*

750-770

Volvo B10M-55   Alexander PS   DP48F   1995

750	M750LAX	755	M755LAX	759	M759LAX	763	M763LAX	767	M767RAX
751	M751LAX	756	M756LAX	760	M760LAX	764	M764LAX	768	M768RAX
752	M752LAX	757	M757LAX	761	M761LAX	765	M765RAX	769	M769RAX
753	M753LAX	758	M758LAX	762	M762LAX	766	M766RAX	770	M770RAX
754	M754LAX								

825	TWS909T	Bristol VRT/SL3/6LXB	Eastern Coach Works	H43/28F	1979	Ex Cheltenham & Gloucester, 1992
827	A541HAC	Leyland Olympian ONLXB/1R	Eastern Coach Works	H43/31F	1983	Ex Midland Red South, 1993
828	A548HAC	Leyland Olympian ONLXB/1R	Eastern Coach Works	H43/31F	1983	Ex Midland Red South, 1993
829	A549HAC	Leyland Olympian ONLXB/1R	Eastern Coach Works	H43/31F	1983	Ex Midland Red South, 1993
830	AET185T	Bristol VRT/SL3/6LXB	Eastern Coach Works	H43/31F	1979	Ex East Midland, 1993
831	DAK201V	Bristol VRT/SL3/501	Eastern Coach Works	H43/31F	1979	Ex East Midland, 1994
832	WAX194S	Bristol VRT/SL3/501(6LXB)	Eastern Coach Works	H43/31F	1977	Ex Ribble, 1994
833	DBV26W	Bristol VRT/SL3/6LXB	Eastern Coach Works	H43/31F	1980	Ex Ribble, 1994

834-844

Bristol VRT/SL3/501   Eastern Coach Works   H43/31F   1980   Ex National Welsh, 1991
836 is fitted with a 6LXB engine

834	BUH232V	836	GTX738W	840	GTX747W	843	GTX750W	844	GTX753W
835	BUH237V	838	GTX743W	841	GTX748W				

845	WAX194S	Bristol VRT/SL3/501(6LXB)	Eastern Coach Works	H43/31F	1977	Ex Ribble, 1994
861	OSR206R	Bristol VRT/LL3/501	Alexander AL	H49/38F	1977	Ex National Welsh, 1991
862	OSR207R	Bristol VRT/LL3/501	Alexander AL	H49/38F	1977	Ex National Welsh, 1991
863	OSR208R	Bristol VRT/LL3/501	Alexander AL	H49/38F	1977	Ex National Welsh, 1991
864	OSR209R	Bristol VRT/LL3/501	Alexander AL	H49/38F	1977	Ex National Welsh, 1991
865	WDA1T	Leyland Titan TNLXB1RF	Park Royal	H43/29F	1978	Ex Selkent, 1994
866	WDA2T	Leyland Titan TNLXB1RF	Park Royal	H43/29F	1979	Ex Selkent, 1994
867	WDA5T	Leyland Titan TNLXB1RF	Park Royal	H43/29F	1979	Ex Selkent, 1994
868	AVK163V	Leyland Atlantean AN68A/2R	Alexander AL	H49/37F	1980	Ex Busways, 1995
869	AVK166V	Leyland Atlantean AN68A/2R	Alexander AL	H49/37F	1980	Ex Busways, 1995
870	AVK173V	Leyland Atlantean AN68A/2R	Alexander AL	H49/37F	1980	Ex Busways, 1995

One of Red and White's surviving Duple Laser bodied Tigers, 925, AKG197A, is pictured in Cardiff heading for Brynmawr, reportedly the highest town in the British Isles. At the time of writing all four of the remaining Lasers were based at Crosskeys depot. *John Jones*

898-915

										Leyland Tiger TRCTL11/3R	Plaxton Paramount 3200	C51F*	1983	Ex National Welsh, 1991

*906-14 are C46F; 915 is C53F

898	AAX450A	901	AAX466A	907	AAL575A	911	AAL516A	914	AAX516A
899	AAX451A	902	AAX488A	909	AAL538A	912	AAX489A	915	AAX529A
900	AAX465A	906	AAL544A	910	AAL518A	913	AAX515A		

916	CYJ492Y	Leyland Tiger TRCTL11/3R	Plaxton Paramount 3200	C50F	1983	Ex Stagecoach South, 1994
917	CYJ493Y	Leyland Tiger TRCTL11/3R	Plaxton Paramount 3200	C50F	1983	Ex Stagecoach South, 1994
925	AKG197A	Leyland Tiger TRCTL11/3R	Duple Laser	C49FT	1984	Ex National Welsh, 1991
927	AKG214A	Leyland Tiger TRCTL11/3R	Duple Laser	C53F	1984	Ex National Welsh, 1991
931	AKG271A	Leyland Tiger TRCTL11/3R	Duple Laser	C49FT	1984	Ex National Welsh, 1991
934	AKG296A	Leyland Tiger TRCTL11/3R	Duple Laser	C53F	1984	Ex National Welsh, 1991
935	A227MDD	Leyland Tiger TRCTL11/3R	Plaxton Paramount 3200	C51F	1984	Ex Cheltenham & Gloucester, 1994

940-951

										Dennis Javelin 11SDA2133	Plaxton Premiére Interurban	DP47F	1994

940	M940JBO	943	M943JBO	946	M946JBO	948	M948JBO	950	M950JBO
941	M941JBO	944	M944JBO	947	M947JBO	949	M949JBO	951	M951JBO
942	M942JBO	945	M945JBO						

952	H159EJU	Dennis Javelin 12SDA1907	Duple 320	C53FT	1991	Ex Whites of Calver, 1995
953	F243OFP	Dennis Javelin 12SDA1907	Duple 320	C53FT	1991	Ex Whites of Calver, 1995
954	HIL8410	Dennis Javelin 12SDA1907	Duple 320	C53FT	1991	Ex Whites of Calver, 1995

Previous Registrations:

A227MDD	A71KDU, 552OHU, A873MRW, YJV806		
AAL516A	SDW927Y	AAX515A	SDW929Y
AAL518A	SDW926Y	AAX516A	SDW930Y
AAL538A	SDW925Y	AAX529A	SDW931Y
AAL544A	SDW922Y	AKG197A	A225VWO
AAL575A	SDW923Y	AKG214A	A227VWO
AAX450A	SDW914Y	AKG271A	A231VWO
AAX451A	SDW915Y	AKG296A	A234VWO
AAX465A	SDW916Y	CYJ492Y	XUF531Y, 401DCD
AAX466A	SDW917Y	CYJ493Y	XUF532Y, 2880CD, 402DCD
AAX488A	SDW918Y	HIL8410	E759JAY
AAX489A	SDW928Y	WAX194S	CBV8S

REES TRAVEL

N A, M E & N A Rees, Waunlapra, Llanelly Hill, Gilwern, Monmouthshire NP7 0PW

BTU636S	Bedford YLQ	Duple Dominant II Express	C45F	1978	Ex Williams, Ponciau, 1982
HUX83V	Bedford YMT	Duple Dominant II Express	C53F	1980	Ex Vagg, Knockin Heath, 1982
HUX84V	Bedford YMT	Duple Dominant II Express	C53F	1980	Ex Vagg, Knockin Heath, 1982
WSV469	DAF SB200SDHU585	Jonckheere Bermuda	C49FT	1982	Ex Drew, Guisborough, 1986
769DAF	DAF EL26/581	Bova Europa	C47FT	1982	Ex Globe, Warmley, 1984
FEV449Y	Bedford YNT	Duple Dominant III	C53F	1982	Ex Stephenson, Hullbridge, 1986
A390VBO	Mercedes-Benz L310	Devon Conversions	M12	1983	Ex Howells, Ynysddu, 1991
RJI8719	Aüwaerter Neoplan N122/3	Aüwaerter Skyliner	CH56/20CT	1983	Ex Brylaine, Boston, 1993
WSV556	DAF SB2300DHS585	Jonckheere Jubilee P50	C51FT	1984	Ex Berryhurst, Vauxhall, 1986
RJI8718	DAF SB2300DHS585	Jonckheere Jubilee P599	C51FT	1984	Ex Berryhurst, Vauxhall, 1988
B292RJF	Bova EL26/581	Bova Europa	C49FT	1985	Ex County, Leicester, 1990
B320RJF	Bova EL26/581	Bova Europa	C49FT	1985	Ex County, Leicester, 1990
F99UNV	LAG G355Z	LAG Panoramic	C49FT	1988	Ex Express Travel, 1994

Previous Registrations:

769DAF	JOU521X	RJI8719	A143RVL, 7878SC, A237VGG
B292RJF	B244YKX, 1661PP	WSV469	DVV538X
B320RJF	B247YKX, 1379PP	WSV556	A160XNV
RJI8718	A150XNH		

Livery: White and two-tone green

Even with four journeys per day from Llanelli Hill to Brynmawr, Rees Travels service barely exceeds 20 miles total each weekday. It is not a particularly demanding service, therefore, except of the nerves as its route includes some precipitous stretches overlooking the stunning Clydach Gorge. Performing the duty here was HUX84V, leaving Brynmawr. *Ian Kirby*

RHONDDA

Rhondda Buses Ltd; Parfitt's Motor Services Ltd, Aberrhondda Road, Porth,
Rhondda Cynon Taff   CF39 0AG

Depots : Bedwas House Ind Est, Bedwas; Aberrhondda Road, Porth and Llechryd Garage, Rhymney Bridge.

16	E316HLO	Mercedes-Benz L307D	Pilcher Green	M12	1988	Ex Parfitt's, 1995
62	N62MTG	Dennis Dart 9.8SDL3054	Plaxton Pointer	B40F	1995	
63	N63MTG	Dennis Dart 9.8SDL3054	Plaxton Pointer	B40F	1995	
64	M64HHB	Dennis Dart 9.8SDL3054	Wright Handy-bus	B39F	1995	
65	M65HHB	Dennis Dart 9.8SDL3054	Wright Handy-bus	B39F	1995	
66	M562JTG	Dennis Dart 9.8SDL3040	Plaxton Pointer	B43F	1994	Ex Parfitt's, 1995
67	M67HHB	Dennis Dart 9.8SDL3054	Wright Handy-bus	B39F	1995	
68	M68HHB	Dennis Dart 9SDL3031	Marshall C36	B34F	1994	
69	M69HHB	Dennis Dart 9SDL3031	Marshall C36	B34F	1994	
70	M625KKG	Dennis Dart 9.8SDL3040	Plaxton Pointer	B43F	1994	Ex Parfitt's, 1995

71-78		Volvo B6-9m		Plaxton Pointer	B35F	1994

71	M71HHB	73	M73HHB	75	M75HHB	76	M76HHB	78	M78HHB
72	M72HHB	74	M74HHB						

79	L79CWO	Volvo B6-9.9M	Plaxton Pointer	B40F	1994
81	L81CWO	Volvo B6-9.9M	Plaxton Pointer	B40F	1994
82	L82CWO	Volvo B6-9.9M	Plaxton Pointer	B40F	1994

The smallest capacity Dennis Darts in the Rhondda fleet are a pair of Marshall-bodied vehicles including 69, M69HHB, allocated to the Caerphilly Busways unit. A new depot has been constructed replacing the premises the unit was sharing with Waddons. The lighter livery scheme employed at Caerphilly is expected to replace the darker scheme for the main fleet which experiences fading and a consequent degradation of appearance.

The shorter, Plaxton-bodied Darts in the fleet now total eight and are thus the more numerous sub-group arising from Rhondda's complicated purchasing policy. Typical of the type is 85, L85CWO passing through Kingsway, Cardiff. *John Jones*

83	L83CWO	Dennis Dart 9SDL3034	Plaxton Pointer	B35F	1993	
84	L84CWO	Dennis Dart 9SDL3034	Plaxton Pointer	B35F	1993	
85	L85CWO	Dennis Dart 9SDL3034	Plaxton Pointer	B35F	1993	
86	L86CWO	Dennis Dart 9SDL3024	Wright Handy-bus	B35F	1993	
87	L87CWO	Dennis Dart 9SDL3024	Wright Handy-bus	B35F	1993	
88	L270EHB	Dennis Dart 9.8SDL3035	Plaxton Pointer	B43F	1994	Ex Parfitt's, 1995
89	L89CWO	Dennis Dart 9SDL3024	Wright Handy-bus	B35F	1993	
90	K402EDT	Dennis Dart 9SDL3016	Northern Counties Paladin	B35F	1992	Ex Mainline, 1996
91	K91BNY	Dennis Dart 9SDL3011	Plaxton Pointer	B35F	1993	
92	K92BNY	Dennis Dart 9SDL3011	Plaxton Pointer	B35F	1993	
93	K93BNY	Dennis Dart 9SDL3011	Plaxton Pointer	B35F	1993	
94	K94AAX	Dennis Dart 9SDL3011	Wright Handy-bus	B35F	1993	
95	K95AAX	Dennis Dart 9SDL3011	Wright Handy-bus	B35F	1993	
96	K96AAX	Dennis Dart 9SDL3016	Plaxton Pointer	B35F	1992	
97	K97XNY	Dennis Dart 9SDL3011	Plaxton Pointer(1995)	B35F	1992	
98	K98XNY	Dennis Dart 9.8SDL3017	Wright Handy-bus	B39F	1992	
99	J454JRH	Dennis Dart 9.8SDL3017	Plaxton Pointer	B40F	1991	Ex Parfitt's, 1995
150	M866LNY	Mercedes-Benz 711D	Plaxton Beaver	B27F	1995	
151	N151MTG	Mercedes-Benz 811D	UVG Citi Star	B33F	1995	

152-160   Mercedes-Benz 711D   UVG Citi Star   B27F   1995

152	N152MTG	154	N154MTG	156	N156MTG	158	N158MTG	160	N160MTG
153	N153MTG	155	N155MTG	157	N157MTG	159	N159MTG		

161-169   Mercedes-Benz 711D   Plaxton Beaver   B27F   1996   161/2 will be 709D

161		163		165		167		169
162		164		166		168		

252	F125YVP	MCW MetroRider MF158/16	MCW	B28F	1988	Ex Stagecoach East London, 1996
253	F815CWJ	MCW MetroRider MF158	MCW	B31F	1988	Ex Stevensons, 1993
254	G689KNW	Optare MetroRider	Optare	B29F	1990	Ex Heaton, Leigh, 1994
255	K320FYG	Optare MetroRider	Optare	B29F	1993	Ex Optare demonstrator, 1994
256	J797MHF	Optare MetroRider	Optare	B29F	1991	Ex Dalybus, Eccles, 1994
257	L839MWT	Optare MetroRider	Optare	B31F	1993	Ex Darlington, 1995
258	L840MWT	Optare MetroRider	Optare	B31F	1993	Ex Darlington, 1995

Rhondda's current minibus choice is the Mercedes-Benz 711D and further examples are due this year. They will replace older MCW MetroRiders in the 2101-26 batch. However, longer and newer Optare MetroRiders such as 258, L840MWT, are expected to be retained. Most of these vehicles are allocated to Parfitts or Caerphilly Busways - the latter operating a Park and Ride contract in Cardiff *(above)*. A number of Leyland Tiger service buses have been accumulated including this ex Nottinghamshire Police prison van thoughtfully rebodied by East Lancashire before entering service with Rhondda. New as G399PNN, 703 is now registered A13RBL. *John Jones*

300	G805XLO	Leyland Swift LBM6T/2RA	Reeve Burgess Harrier	B41F	1989	Ex LB Hillingdon, 1995
301	E308HPU	Leyland Swift LBM6T/2RA	Wadham Stringer Vanguard	B37F	1988	Ex Harris Bus, West Thurrock, 1995
302	E309HPU	Leyland Swift LBM6T/2RA	Wadham Stringer Vanguard	B37F	1988	Ex Harris Bus, West Thurrock, 1995
371w	GGM71W	Leyland Leopard PSU3F/4R	Plaxton Supreme IV Express	C49F	1981	Ex Parfitt's, 1995
372	VEG155S	Leyland Leopard PSU3E/4R	Plaxton Supreme III Express	C53F	1978	Ex Parfitt's, 1995
373w	GGM73W	Leyland Leopard PSU3F/4R	Plaxton Supreme IV Express	C49F	1981	Ex Parfitt's, 1995
375	KUX230W	Leyland Leopard PSU5D/4R	Duple Dominant IV	C57F	1980	Ex Parfitt's, 1995
376	JNB150N	Leyland Leopard PSU3C/4R	Duple Dominant	C53F	1975	Ex Classic, Annfield Plain, 1996
383	BYW383V	Leyland National 10351A/2R		B44F	1979	Ex Parfitt's, 1995
393w	BYW393V	Leyland National 10351A/2R(DAF)		B44F	1979	Ex Parfitt's, 1995
397	BYW397V	Leyland National 10351A/2R		B44F	1979	Ex Parfitt's, 1995
475	YBO150T	Leyland National 10351A/1R		B44F	1979	Ex TGM Buses, Cardiff, 1992
478	YDW400T	Leyland National 10351A/1R		B44F	1979	Ex TGM Buses, Cardiff, 1992
500	E62WDT	Leyland Lynx LX112TL11ZR1R	Leyland Lynx	B49F	1987	Ex Chesterfield, 1994
502	E63WDT	Leyland Lynx LX112TL11ZR1R	Leyland Lynx	B49F	1987	Ex The Birmingham Coach Co, 1994
550	N550MTG	Mercedes-Benz 0405	Optare Prisma	B49F	1995	
551	N551MTG	Mercedes-Benz 0405	Optare Prisma	B49F	1995	
696	B26ADW	Leyland Tiger TRBTL11/2RP	East Lancashire	DP47F	1984	Ex TGM Buses, Cardiff 1992
697	B27ADW	Leyland Tiger TRBTL11/2RP	East Lancashire	DP47F	1984	Ex TGM Buses, Cardiff 1992
698	EWR656Y	Leyland Tiger TRBTL11/2R	Duple Dominant	DP47F	1983	Ex Rider Group, 1996
699	EWR657Y	Leyland Tiger TRBTL11/2R	Duple Dominant	DP47F	1983	Ex Rider Group, 1996
700	A17RBL	Leyland Tiger TRBTL11/2RP	Duple Dominant	B55F	1988	Ex Kelvin Central, 1994
701	A19RBL	Leyland Tiger TRBTL11/2RP	Plaxton Derwent II	B54F	1988	Ex Thames Transit, 1994
702	A20RBL	Leyland Tiger TRBTL11/2RP	Plaxton Derwent II	B54F	1988	Ex Thames Transit, 1994
703	A13RBL	Leyland Tiger TRBL10/2RZA	East Lancashire (1995)	DP53F	1990	Ex Nottinghamshire Police, 1995
704	A14RBL	Volvo Citybus B10M-50	East Lancashire (1995)	DP53F	1984	Ex Western Scottish, 1995
705	A15RBL	Volvo B10M-56	Van Hool Alizée L	B51F	1994	Ex Henderson, Blantyre, 1995
717	GTX741W	Bristol VRT/SL3/501	Eastern Coach Works	H43/31F	1980	Ex TGM Buses, Cardiff, 1992
850	HIL3188	Leyland Olympian ONTL11/2RH	East Lancashire	CH47/31F	1987	Ex Rossendale, 1995
851	F50ACL	Volvo Citybus B10M-50	Alexander RV	H47/35F	1989	Ex Great Yarmouth, 1995
852	F51ACL	Volvo Citybus B10M-50	Alexander RV	H47/35F	1989	Ex Great Yarmouth, 1995
900	YLP528	Volvo B10M-61	Van Hool Alizée	C51FT	1983	Ex Cardiff Bluebird, 1994
902	NIW8291	Leyland Tiger TRCTL11/3RZ	Van Hool Alizée	C53F	1986	Ex Parfitt's, 1995
903	AAL622A	Leyland Tiger TRCTL11/3R	Plaxton Paramount 3200	C51F	1983	Ex TGM Buses, Cardiff, 1992
904	AAL587A	Leyland Tiger TRCTL11/3R	Plaxton Paramount 3200	C51F	1983	Ex TGM Buses, Cardiff, 1992
905	NIW2309	Leyland Tiger TRCTL11/3R	Van Hool Alizée	C51FT	1984	Ex Parfitt's, 1995
906	NIW4810	Leyland Tiger TRCTL11/3R	Plaxton Paramount 3200	C57F	1984	Ex Parfitt's, 1995
909	B973OSB	Dennis DorchesterSDA810	Plaxton Paramount 3500 II	C46FT	1985	Ex Clydeside, 1996

2101-2117		MCW MetroRider MF150/104*	MCW	DP25F	1988	Ex TGM Buses, Cardiff, 1992
						*2106-17 are MF150/103

2101	F101YWO	2106	F106YWO	2109	F109YWO	2112	F112YWO	2116	F116YWO
2104	F104YWO	2107	F107YWO	2110	F110YWO	2114	F114YWO	2117	F117YWO
2105	F105YWO	2108	F108YWO						

2118	D473PON	MCW MetroRider MF150/14	MCW	B23F	1987	Ex London Buses, 1992
2122	E128KYW	MCW MetroRider MF150/38	MCW	B25F	1987	Ex Cyril Evans, 1993
2124	D472PON	MCW MetroRider MF150/14	MCW	B23F	1987	Ex Cyril Evans, 1993
2125	D479PON	MCW MetroRider MF150/18	MCW	DP23F	1987	Ex Parfitt's, 1995
2126	D481PON	MCW MetroRider MF150/18	MCW	DP23F	1987	Ex Parfitt's, 1995

Previous Registrations:

A13RBL	G399PNN	AAL622A	SDW919Y
A14RBL	B176FFS, WLT444, B660EGG	B973OSB	B405OSB, 705DYE, B983EGG, WLT364
A15RBL	B947ASU	HIL3188	D888YHG
A17RBL	F311RMH	NIW2309	A381ROU, JEP597, A574AHB
A19RBL	F603CET	NIW4810	A943XDW, JEP417, A573AHB
A20RBL	F604CET	NIW8291	C341DND
AAL587A	SDW920Y	YLP526	MSU571Y

Livery:

	Maroon, cream and red or maroon and cream
Caerphilly Busways	68/9/71/3-6/97, 156-60, 253/4, 397, 475, 2105/10/22/4
Parfitt's	16, 62/3/6/70/88, 252/5-8, 300-2/71-3/5/93, 696/7, 900/2/5/6, 2125/6
Rhondda	Remainder

Page 85 bottom: **The original Rhondda Transport Company built up a large double decker fleet from the 1930s and regular intakes of AEC Regents continued until 1966. Nowadays, however, only four Rhondda deckers are operated, including a pair of Alexander bodied Volvo Citybuss purchased from Great Yarmouth in 1995. Number 852, F51ACL, is seen in High Street, Cardiff.** *John Jones*

SHAMROCK

A Jones, 34 Taff Street, Pontypridd, Rhondda Cynon Taff   CF37 3JP

Depots :Pontcynon Ind Est, Abercynon; Cardiff Road, Cadoxton, Barry and Stephenson Road Ind Est, Newport

XDL794L	Leyland National 1151/1R/0501		B46D	1973	Ex Gary's, Tredegar, 1994
NHA259M	Leyland National 1151/2R/2801		B51F	1973	Ex Dunn-Line, Nottingham, 1994
KSO64P	Leyland National 10351/2R		B40D	1976	Ex Gary's, Tredegar, 1994
KJD542P	Leyland National 10351A/2R		B36D	1976	Ex Westbus, Ashford, 1993
PKG739R	Leyland National 11351A/1R		B49F	1976	Ex Phil Anslow Travel, 1993
RHB305R	Leyland National 10351A/1R		B41F	1977	Ex Thomas of Barry, 1996
SKG906S	Leyland National 11351A/1R		B49F	1976	Ex Phil Anslow Travel, 1993
THX191S	Leyland National 10351A/2R		B44F	1978	Ex London Buses, 1992
THX213S	Leyland National 10351A/2R(Volvo)		B44F	1978	Ex Glyn Williams, Crosskeys, 1995
THX218S	Leyland National 10351A/2R		B44F	1978	Ex London Buses, 1992
VHB673S	Bristol VRT/SL3/501	Eastern Coach Works	H43/31F	1978	Ex Cynon Valley, 1992
XWX172S	Leyland Leopard PSU3E/4R	Duple Dominant II	C53F	1978	Ex Glyn Williams, Crosskeys, 1993
YYE282T	Leyland National 10351A/2R		B36D	1978	Ex Westbus, Ashford, 1993
AYR349T	Leyland National 10351A/2R		B44F	1979	Ex Glyn Williams, Crosskeys, 1995
SWP888V	Leyland Leopard PSU5C/4R	Duple Dominant II	C57F	1979	Ex Glyn Williams, Crosskeys, 1993
DDW530V	Bedford YMT	Duple Dominant II	C53F	1979	Ex Thomas of Barry, 1996
A447PFO	Bedford YNT	Plaxton Paramount 3200	C53F	1983	Ex Jones Motors, Ynysybwl, 1989
680XAE	Volvo B10M-61	Plaxton Paramount 3500 II	C49F	1986	Ex Thomas of Barry, 1996
TIB1224	Volvo B10M-61	Caetano Algarve	C49FT	1986	Ex Thomas of Barry, 1996
C330MLG	Mercedes-Benz L608D	PMT Hanbridge	B20F	1986	
C327UFP	Mercedes-Benz L608D	Reeve Burgess	B20F	1986	
C328UFP	Mercedes-Benz L608D	Reeve Burgess	B20F	1986	

Opposite, top: **Mercedes-Benz has been the main source of new midibuses for Shamrock for ten years, and eight L608Ds purchased in 1986 are still in use. Around sixty of this marque are now in service and one of the latest batch, N857PDW, a 711D with LCB Eagle bodywork is seen swinging into the bus station in Cardiff.** *Les Peters*

Opposite, bottom: **One of the post-deregulation success stories is undoubtedly Shamrock, with a fleet strength now in excess of one hundred and thirty vehicles. In less than two years, twenty one new Dennis Darts have entered service with bodywork divided between Plaxton, Northern Counties and Marshall. One of the latter, N513PNY, is seen leaving Pontypridd on a former National Welsh route.** *John Jones*

Shamrock's sole double decker is this former National Welsh Bristol VR, VHB673S. It is employed, almost exclusively, on school contracts and was laying over at Pontypridd bus station when photographed. Shamrock have been very successful in gaining such work in the last two years and the expanded fleet of contract vehicles demonstrates this. *John Jones*

The South Wales Bus Handbook

D985ARE	Mercedes-Benz L608D	Sparshatt	B20F	1986	
D986ARE	Mercedes-Benz L608D	Sparshatt	B20F	1986	
D987ARE	Mercedes-Benz L608D	Advanced Vehicle Bodies	B20F	1986	
D989ARE	Mercedes-Benz L608D	Advanced Vehicle Bodies	B20F	1986	
PNH182	Volvo B10M-61	Plaxton Paramount 3500 III	C49FT	1987	Ex Thomas of Barry, 1996
D362SDM	Mercedes-Benz 709D	PMT	B19F	1987	
D363SDM	Mercedes-Benz 709D	PMT	B20F	1987	
D879UFJ	Mercedes-Benz 609D	Reeve Burgess	B20F	1987	
LIL9969	Leyland Tiger TRCTL11/3RZ	Plaxton Paramount 3200 III	C55F	1987	Ex Trumans, New Inn, 1996
LIL9970	Leyland Tiger TRCTL11/3RZ	Plaxton Paramount 3200 III	C55F	1988	Ex Trumans, New Inn, 1996
LIL9971	Dennis Javelin 12SDA1907	Duple 320	C57F	1988	
E918AFM	Mercedes-Benz 609D	Advanced Vehicle Bodies	C24F	1988	
E807FRY	Mercedes-Benz 709D	Reeve Burgess Beaver	B25F	1988	
F210AKG	Freight Rover Sherpa	Carlyle Citybus 2	B20F	1988	Ex National Welsh, 1992
F112AHB	Mercedes-Benz 709D	Reeve Burgess Beaver	B25F	1988	
F113AHB	Mercedes-Benz 709D	Reeve Burgess Beaver	B25F	1988	
LIL9972	Dennis Javelin 12SDA1907	Duple 320	C55F	1988	
F427EMB	Mercedes-Benz 609D	PMT	B20F	1988	
F428EMB	Mercedes-Benz 609D	PMT	B24F	1988	
F961XWM	Mercedes-Benz 609D	North West Coach Sales	B20F	1988	
F962XWM	Mercedes-Benz 609D	North West Coach Sales	B20F	1988	
F963XWM	Mercedes-Benz 609D	Robin Hood	B20F	1988	
F964XWM	Mercedes-Benz 609D	North West Coach Sales	B20F	1988	
LIL9975	Leyland Tiger TRCL10/3ARZM	Plaxton Paramount 3500 III	C53FT	1989	Ex Hill's of Tredegar, 1992
LIL9976	Leyland Tiger TRCL10/3ARZM	Plaxton Paramount 3500 III	C49FT	1989	Ex Hill's of Tredegar, 1992
F670DBO	Mercedes-Benz 811D	Reeve Burgess Beaver	B33F	1989	
F671DBO	Mercedes-Benz 811D	Reeve Burgess Beaver	B33F	1989	
F672DBO	Mercedes-Benz 811D	Reeve Burgess Beaver	B33F	1989	
F664TBE	Mercedes-Benz 811D	Coachcraft	C24F	1989	Ex B&D Richards, Cimla, 1993
LIL9973	Dennis Javelin 12SDA1907	Duple 320	C57F	1989	
LIL9974	Dennis Javelin 12SDA1907	Duple 320	C57F	1989	
G370CAJ	CVE Omni	CVE	B23F	1989	Ex CVE demonstrator, 1991
G654EVN	CVE Omni	CVE	B23F	1989	Ex CVE demonstrator, 1990
G841CLV	Mercedes-Benz 609D	North West Coach Sales	B20F	1989	
G847VAY	Dennis Javelin 11SDL1909	Duple 300	B55F	1989	
G40HDW	Freight Rover Sherpa	Carlyle Citybus 2	B20F	1990	Ex Bebb, Llantwit Fardre, 1992
H368NDW	Dennis Javelin 12SDA1919	Duple 320	C57F	1990	
H787NUH	Mercedes-Benz 811D	Reeve Burgess Beaver	B33F	1990	
H788NUH	Mercedes-Benz 811D	Reeve Burgess Beaver	B33F	1990	
H789NUH	Mercedes-Benz 811D	Reeve Burgess Beaver	B33F	1990	
H492OHB	Mercedes-Benz 811D	Reeve Burgess Beaver	B31F	1990	
H493OHB	Mercedes-Benz 811D	Reeve Burgess Beaver	B33F	1990	
H494OHB	Mercedes-Benz 811D	Reeve Burgess Beaver	B33F	1990	
H687UHH	Mercedes-Benz 709D	Made-to-Measure	B28F	1991	
H688UHH	Mercedes-Benz 709D	Made-to-Measure	B28F	1991	
H689UHH	Mercedes-Benz 709D	Made-to-Measure	B28F	1991	
H690UHH	Mercedes-Benz 709D	Made-to-Measure	B28F	1991	
J174GGG	Mercedes-Benz 609D	Made-to-Measure	C26F	1991	Ex Steve Lynch, Magor, 1994
K927AEP	Mercedes-Benz 811D	Dormobile Routemaker	DP33F	1992	
K928AEP	Mercedes-Benz 811D	Dormobile Routemaker	DP33F	1992	
K929AEP	Mercedes-Benz 811D	Dormobile Routemaker	DP33F	1992	
K930AEP	Mercedes-Benz 811D	Dormobile Routemaker	DP33F	1992	
K365TJF	Mercedes-Benz 811D	Dormobile Routemaker	DP33F	1992	
K366TJF	Mercedes-Benz 811D	Dormobile Routemaker	DP33F	1992	
K586MHY	Mercedes-Benz 709D	Dormobile Routemaker	B27F	1993	
K588MHY	Mercedes-Benz 709D	Dormobile Routemaker	B27F	1993	
K589TRY	Mercedes-Benz 814D	Dormobile Routemaker	DP33F	1993	
K590TRY	Mercedes-Benz 814D	Dormobile Routemaker	DP33F	1993	
K451VAY	Bluebird Q Bus	Bluebird	DP31F	1992	Ex Bluebird demonstrator, 1993
L465XNR	Mercedes-Benz 811D	Dormobile Routemaker	B33F	1993	
L466XNR	Mercedes-Benz 811D	Dormobile Routemaker	B33F	1993	
L467XNR	Mercedes-Benz 811D	Dormobile Routemaker	B33F	1993	
L468XNR	Mercedes-Benz 811D	Dormobile Routemaker	B33F	1993	
L536XNR	Mercedes-Benz 811D	Dormobile Routemaker	B33F	1993	
L537XNR	Mercedes-Benz 811D	Dormobile Routemaker	B33F	1993	
L552XNR	Mercedes-Benz 811D	Dormobile Routemaker	B33F	1993	
L553XNR	Mercedes-Benz 811D	Dormobile Routemaker	B33F	1993	
L361ANR	Mercedes-Benz 811D	Dormobile Routemaker	B33F	1993	
L362ANR	Mercedes-Benz 811D	Dormobile Routemaker	B33F	1993	
L38DBC	Dennis Javelin 12SDA2136	Caetano Algarve II	C55F	1994	
L957JGS	Iveco TurboCity 480.10.21	WS Vanguard II	B47F	1994	
L775GNM	Iveco TurboCity 480.10.21	WS Vanguard II	B47F	1994	
M851JHB	Dennis Dart 9.8SDL3040	Plaxton Pointer	B40F	1994	

The South Wales Bus Handbook

Extensive road works in Pontypridd over the last two years has caused much disruption to bus services and many were re-scheduled to allow for this. Now that the new inner relief road is virtually completed a lot of improvements can be made to journey times. *Above* Northern Counties Paladin-bodied Dennis Dart, M983KKG, manoeuvres around residual work-in-progress in this view by Pontypridd Station. *Below* Shamrock were particularly pleased with the performance of their first Bluebird Q Bus which arrived in 1993 and immediately ordered more, both short and long-wheelbase versions. Delays in availability of right hand drive models however has meant only one of the later has actually been received and M31KUT was photographed immediately after delivery. *John Jones*

M852JHB	Dennis Dart 9.8SDL3040	Plaxton Pointer	B40F	1994
M737JKG	Dennis Dart 9.8SDL3040	Plaxton Pointer	B40F	1994
M738JKG	Dennis Dart 9.8SDL3040	Plaxton Pointer	B40F	1994
M425JNY	Dennis Dart 9.8SDL3040	Plaxton Pointer	B40F	1994
M426JNY	Dennis Dart 9.8SDL3040	Plaxton Pointer	B40F	1994
M710HBC	Dennis Javelin 12SDA2131	Plaxton Premiére 320	C53F	1995
M711HBC	Dennis Javelin 12SDA2131	Plaxton Premiére 320	C53F	1995
M982KKG	Dennis Dart 9.8SDL3054	Northern Counties Paladin	B40F	1995
M983KKG	Dennis Dart 9.8SDL3054	Northern Counties Paladin	B40F	1995
M984KKG	Dennis Dart 9.8SDL3054	Northern Counties Paladin	B40F	1995
M985KKG	Dennis Dart 9.8SDL3054	Northern Counties Paladin	B40F	1995
M986KKG	Dennis Dart 9.8SDL3054	Northern Counties Paladin	B40F	1995
M987KKG	Dennis Dart 9.8SDL3054	Northern Counties Paladin	B40F	1995
M252KNR	Mercedes-Benz 709D	Alexander Sprint	B29F	1995
M31KUT	Bluebird Q Bus	Bluebird	DP47F	1995
N755NAY	Dennis Javelin 12SDA2136	Marcopolo Explorer	C53F	1995
N461OTX	Dennis Dart 9.8SDL3054	Marshall C37	B40F	1995
N462OTX	Dennis Dart 9.8SDL3054	Marshall C37	B40F	1995
N463OTX	Dennis Dart 9.8SDL3054	Marshall C37	B40F	1995
N511PNY	Dennis Dart 9.8SDL3054	Marshall C37	B40F	1996
N512PNY	Dennis Dart 9.8SDL3054	Marshall C37	B40F	1996
N513PNY	Dennis Dart 9.8SDL3054	Marshall C37	B40F	1996
N143XEG	Dennis Dart 9.8SDL3054	Marshall C37	B40F	1996
N144XEG	Dennis Dart 9.8SDL3054	Marshall C37	B40F	1996
N145XEG	Dennis Dart 9.8SDL3054	Marshall C37	B40F	1996
N854PDW	Mercedes-Benz 711D	LCB Eagle 29	B29F	1996
N855PDW	Mercedes-Benz 711D	LCB Eagle 29	B29F	1996
N856PDW	Mercedes-Benz 711D	LCB Eagle 29	B29F	1996
N857PDW	Mercedes-Benz 711D	LCB Eagle 29	B29F	1996

Previous Registrations:

680XAE	C122DWR, 904DRH	LIL9972	F106AKG	LIL9976	F599BTG
A447PFO	A411OFO	LIL9973	F632SAY	PNH182	D875EEH
LIL9969	E969NMK	LIL9974	F631SAY	TIB1224	D213VVV
LIL9970	E973NMK	LIL9975	F593BTG	TYW679	LBO12X
LIL9971	E726UHB				

Livery: White, yellow and green or white and yellow; cream and red (Thomas of Barry)

Always alive to a good deal, Shamrock took advantage of the availability of a batch of Italian-built Iveco TurboCity saloons bodied by WS Coachbuilders, successors to Wadham Stringer and now, UVG. This batch imported by Ratby-based dealer Alan Wilson is now spread widely and Shamrocks pair including L775GNM seen here see regular use.
John Jones

The South Wales Bus Handbook

SILVERLINE

W M A Howarth, c/o Davies Transport, The Willows, Abercanaid, Merthyr Tydfil   CF48 1ST

D896NUA	Volkswagen LT55	Optare City Pacer	C21F	1987	
D901MWR	Volkswagen LT55	Optare City Pacer	DP21F	1987	Ex Patterson, Birmngham, 1993
E961PME	Leyland Swift LBM6T/2RS	Wadham Stringer Vanguard	B37F	1988	Ex Jersey Motor Transport, 1989
L965DBO	Dennis Javelin 11SDL 2130	Wadham Stringer Vanguard II	DP49F	1993	
L414SFL	Dennis Dart 9.8SDL3034	Marshall C37	DP37F	1994	
N859PDY	Mercedes-Benz 811D	UVG UrbanStar	DP29F	1996	

Previous Registrations:
E961PME   E961PME,J45700

Livery: Blue and silver

Silverlines interesting fleet of vehicles are worked very hard on a tightly scheduled group of interworked services linking Merthyr Tydfil, Brecon, Swansea and the communities in the Swansea Valley.

Left: The largest vehicle is currently **L965DBO, a Dennis Javelin with Wadham Stringer bodywork similar to the large numbers supplied to the MOD.** *Lower,left:* Newly into service, and yet to receive fleetnames when photographed, is **N859PDY the operators first Mercedes-Benz here with UVG UrbanStar bodywork.** *Byron Gage*

SWT

South Wales Transport Co Ltd, Heol Gwyrosydd, Penlan, Swansea, SA5 7BN

Part of FirstBus plc
Depots: Withybush Industrial Estate, Haverfordwest; Inkerman Street, Llanelli; Tawe Terrace, Pontardawe; Pentregethin Road, Ravenhill, Swansea and Pontardulais Road, Tycroes. **Outstations:** Carmarthen, Ludchurch, Neath and Pembroke Dock

102	J2SWT	Volvo B10M-60	Plaxton Expressliner 2	C46FT	1992	
103	J3SWT	Volvo B10M-60	Plaxton Expressliner 2	C46FT	1992	
104	J4SWT	Volvo B10M-60	Plaxton Expressliner 2	C46FT	1992	
105	J5SWT	Volvo B10M-60	Plaxton Expressliner 2	C46FT	1992	
106	L506GEP	Volvo B10M-60	Plaxton Expressliner 2	C46FT	1993	
107	M107NEP	Dennis Javelin GX 12SDA2132	Plaxton Expressliner 2	C44FT	1994	
108	M108NEP	Dennis Javelin GX 12SDA2132	Plaxton Expressliner 2	C44FT	1994	
109	M109PWN	Dennis Javelin GX 12SDA2133	Plaxton Expressliner 2	C44FT	1995	
110	M110PWN	Dennis Javelin GX 12SDA2133	Plaxton Expressliner 2	C44FT	1995	
111	M111PWN	Dennis Javelin GX 12SDA2133	Plaxton Expressliner 2	C44FT	1995	
112	N112EWJ	Dennis Javelin GX 12SDA2153	Plaxton Expressliner 2	C44FT	1996	
113	N113VWN	Dennis Javelin GX 12SDA2153	Plaxton Expressliner 2	C46FT	1996	
114	N114VWN	Dennis Javelin GX 12SDA2153	Plaxton Expressliner 2	C46FT	1996	
115	N115VWN	Dennis Javelin GX 12SDA2153	Plaxton Expressliner 2	C46FT	1996	
131	C312KTH	Hestair-Duple SDA1510	Duple 425	C53FT	1986	
132	ACY178A	Hestair-Duple SDA1510	Duple 425	C48FT	1986	
133	MKH487A	Hestair-Duple SDA1510	Duple 425	C48FT	1986	
134	F134DEP	Hestair-Duple SDA1510	Duple 425	C48FT	1989	
135	F135DEP	Hestair-Duple SDA1510	Duple 425	C48FT	1989	
136	F99CEP	Hestair-Duple SDA1510	Duple 425	C46FT	1989	Ex United Welsh Coaches, 1989
137	F100CEP	Hestair-Duple SDA1512	Duple 425	C46FT	1989	Ex Brewers, 1989
139	E206BOD	Hestair-Duple SDA1510	Duple 425	C53FT	1988	Ex Brewers, 1995

215-253		Mercedes-Benz L608D	Robin Hood	B20F*	1985-86 *220 is DP19F

215	C215HTH	226	D226LCY	234	D234LCY	241	D241LCY	248	D248LCY
220	D220LCY	227	D227LCY	235	D235LCY	242	D242LCY	249	D249LCY
221	D221LCY	228	D228LCY	236	D236LCY	243	D243LCY	250	D250LCY
222	D222LCY	229	D229LCY	237	D237LCY	244	D244LCY	251	D251LCY
223	D223LCY	230	D230LCY	238	D238LCY	245	D245LCY	252	D252LCY
224	D224LCY	232	D232LCY	239	D239LCY	246	D246LCY	253	D253LCY
225	D225LCY	233	D233LCY	240	D240LCY	247	D247LCY		

SWT have been progressively replacing their Volvo/Expressliners with Dennis Javelin GX-based versions. The GX-variant, while also fitted with a Cummins C-series engine, delivers some 290bhp, considerably more than the standard and comparable to the larger engined heavyweights. SWTs, 110, M110PWN, is seen in Cardiff in full Air Link livery. *John Jones*

SWTs 328, F328FCY, waits time aside Tenby's town walls on a bright day early in 1996. The limitations of area marketing names become obvious when you realise that the nearest city to Tenby is St Davids - not Swansea for whom the City Mini scheme was designed. *John Jones*

279	E279TTH			Mercedes-Benz 609D		Robin Hood		B20F	1987	
280	E280TTH			Mercedes-Benz 609D		Robin Hood		B20F	1987	
281	E281TTH			Mercedes-Benz 609D		Robin Hood		B20F	1987	
282	E282TTH			Mercedes-Benz 609D		Robin Hood		B20F	1987	

287-322

Mercedes-Benz 709D   Reeve Burgess Beaver   B25F*   1988   287/9 ex Brewers, 1994; *304 is DP25F

287	E287UCY	296	E296VEP	303	E303VEP	310	F310AWN	317	F317AWN
289	E289VEP	297	E297VEP	304	E304VEP	311	F311AWN	318	F318AWN
290	E290VEP	298	E298VEP	305	E305VEP	312	F312AWN	319	F319AWN
291	E291VEP	299	E299VEP	306	E306VEP	313	F313AWN	320	F320AWN
292	E292VEP	300	E300VEP	307	F307AWN	314	F314AWN	321	F321AWN
293	E293VEP	301	E301VEP	308	F308AWN	315	F315AWN	322	F322AWN
295	E295VEP	302	E302VEP	309	F309AWN	316	F316AWN		

323-327

Mercedes-Benz 811D   Reeve Burgess Beaver   B25F   1989   Ex Brewers, 1994

323	F323DCY	324	F324DCY	325	F325DCY	326	F326DCY	327	F327DCY

328-347

Mercedes-Benz 814D   Robin Hood   B31F   1989

328	F328FCY	332	F332FCY	336	F336FCY	340	F340FCY	344	G344GEP
329	F329FCY	333	F333FCY	337	F337FCY	341	F341FCY	345	G345GEP
330	F330FCY	334	F334FCY	338	F338FCY	342	F342FCY	346	G346GEP
331	F331FCY	335	F335FCY	339	F339FCY	343	F343FCY	347	G347GEP

Only three second-hand Mercedes-Benz minibuses break the strangle hold of two families of bodybuilders in the SWT fleet. With the vast majority carrying Robin Hood/Phoenix or Reeve Burgess/Plaxton bodies a fair degree of standardisation has been achieved. Reeve Burgess bodywork features on 302, E302VEP seen passing Swansea Castle. *John Jones*

348-361
Mercedes-Benz 814D   Phoenix B31F   1989

348	G348JTH	351	G351JTH	354	G354JTH	357	G357JTH	360	G360JTH
349	G349JTH	352	G352JTH	355	G355JTH	358	G358JTH	361	G361JTH
350	G350JTH	353	G353JTH	356	G356JTH	359	G359JTH		

365-371
Mercedes-Benz 814D   Phoenix   B31F*   1990   *367-70 are DP31F

365	G365JTH	367	G367MEP	369	G369MEP	370	G370MEP	371	G371MEP
366	G366JTH	368	G368MEP						

372	G372MEP	Mercedes-Benz 814D	Plaxton Beaver (1992)	B31F	1990

373-381
Mercedes-Benz 814D   Phoenix   B31F   1990

373	G373MEP	375	H375OTH	377	H377OTH	379	H379OTH	381	H381OTH
374	H374OTH	376	H376OTH	378	H378OTH	380	H380OTH		

382	H382TTH	Mercedes-Benz 814D	Reeve Burgess Beaver	B31F	1991	
383	M997CYS	Mercedes-Benz 811D	WS Wessex II	B31F	1994	Ex Pullman, Crofty, 1995
384	L364GTH	Mercedes-Benz 609D	Cymric	B22F	1993	Ex Rees & Williams, 1996
385	H852OWN	Mercedes-Benz 811D	Reeve Burgess Beaver	B31F	1990	Ex Rees & Williams, 1996
386	H853OWN	Mercedes-Benz 811D	Reeve Burgess Beaver	B31F	1990	Ex Rees & Williams, 1996
387	D31MWN	Mercedes-Benz 609D	Made-to-Measure	C27F	1986	Ex Rees & Williams, 1996
395	J581VTH	Dennis Dart 9.8SDL3012	Plaxton Pointer	B40F	1992	Ex Rees & Williams, 1996
396	J582VTH	Dennis Dart 9.8SDL3012	Plaxton Pointer	B40F	1992	Ex Rees & Williams, 1996
397	J580VTH	Dennis Dart 9.8SDL3012	Plaxton Pointer	B40F	1992	Ex Rees & Williams, 1996
398	L844JCY	Dennis Dart 9.8SDL3035	Plaxton Pointer	B40F	1994	Ex Rees & Williams, 1996
399	K82BWN	Dennis Dart 9.8SDL3017	Alexander Dash	B40F	1993	Ex Rees & Williams, 1996
500	WNO484	Bristol KSW5G	Eastern Coach Works	O33/28R	1953	Ex Eastern National, 1974

SWT were amongst the first National Express contractors to deliberately avoid the Volvo/Plaxton domination of the express coach market. Early experience with the Duple 425 convinced SWT that the frugal, yet reliable, Cummins C-series engine provided positive benefits. The brief flirtation with standard Expressliners in 1992/93 has now given way to Cummins-powered Javelins. *Above* Oldest of the Duple 425s, 131, C312KTH, is now a regular on the Swansea-Cardiff shuttle. *Below* Cummins power is also found in a batch of 1985 Olympians including 907, C907FCY seen here in Swansea city centre. *John Jones*

A third successive batch of Dennis Darts arrived in late 1995 and these retain SWT-specification capacity of 31-seated passengers for operational reasons. *Above* Bearing standard City Mini fleetnames, 556, N556UCY, negotiates the increasingly bus-friendly road environment in Swansea. The main event since the last book has been the acquisition by SWT of D Coaches' Rees & Williams business. This involved the transfer of Rees & Williams Darts and minibuses but the large number of elderly Leopards were replaced by Nationals from SWT's fellow FirstBus subsidiary, Thamesway and the return of others previously cascaded to Brewers including 802, TWN802S. *John Jones/Steve Powell*

501-524   Dennis Dart 9SDL3034   Plaxton Pointer   B31F   1993

501	L501HCY	506	L506HCY	511	L511HCY	516	L516HCY	521	L521HCY
502	L502HCY	507	L507HCY	512	L512HCY	517	L517HCY	522	L522HCY
503	L503HCY	508	L508HCY	513	L513HCY	518	L518HCY	523	L523HCY
504	L504HCY	509	L509HCY	514	L514HCY	519	L519HCY	524	L524HCY
505	L505HCY	510	L510HCY	515	L515HCY	520	L520HCY		

525-550   Dennis Dart 9SDL3034   Plaxton Pointer   B31F   1994

525	L525JEP	531	L531JEP	536	L536JEP	541	L541JEP	546	L546JEP
526	L526JEP	532	L532JEP	537	L537JEP	542	L542JEP	547	L547JEP
527	L527JEP	533	L533JEP	538	L538JEP	543	L543JEP	548	L548JEP
528	L528JEP	534	L534JEP	539	L539JEP	544	L544JEP	549	L549JEP
529	L529JEP	535	L535JEP	540	L540JEP	545	L545JEP	550	L550JEP
530	L530JEP								

551-568   Dennis Dart 9SDL3034   Plaxton Pointer   B31F   1995

551	N551UCY	555	N555UCY	559	N559UCY	563	N563UCY	566	N566UCY
552	N552UCY	556	N556UCY	561	N561UCY	564	N564UCY	567	N567UCY
553	N553UCY	557	N557UCY	562	N562UCY	565	N565UCY	568	N568UCY
554	N554UCY	558	N558UCY						

607	F607AWN	Mercedes-Benz 709D	Reeve Burgess Beaver	DP25F	1988	
792	OEP792R	Leyland National 11351A/1R		B49F	1976	Ex Brewers, 1995
802	TWN802S	Leyland National 11351A/1R		B49F	1978	Ex Brewers, 1995
804	WWN804T	Leyland National 11351A/1R		B49F	1979	Ex Brewers, 1995
805	WWN805T	Leyland National 11351A/1R		B49F	1979	Ex Brewers, 1995
813	AWN813V	Leyland National 11351A/1R		B49F	1979	
815	AWN815V	Leyland National 11351A/1R		B52F	1979	

816-825   Dennis Lance 11SDA3112   Plaxton Verde   DP45F   1993

816	L816HCY	818	L818HCY	820	L820HCY	822	L822HCY	824	L824HCY
817	L817HCY	819	L819HCY	821	L821HCY	823	L823HCY	825	L825HCY

901-907   Leyland Olympian ONCL10/1RV   Eastern Coach Works   H45/30F   1985

901	C901FCY	903	C903FCY	905	C905FCY	906	C906FCY	907	C907FCY
902	C902FCY	904	C904FCY						

908	IIL1828	Leyland Olympian ONTL11/2RSp	Eastern Coach Works	CH45/28F	1985	Ex Thamesway, 1991
909	IIL1829	Leyland Olympian ONTL11/2RSp	Eastern Coach Works	CH45/28F	1985	Ex Thamesway, 1991

975-995   Bristol VRT/SL3/501   Eastern Coach Works   H43/31F   1979-80

975	BEP975V	980	BEP980V	989	ECY989V	992	EWN992W	995	EWN995W
976	BEP976V	984	BEP984V	991	ECY991V	994	EWN994W		

1853-1909   Leyland National 11351A/1R   B49F   1978-79 Ex Thamesway, 1995

1853	YEV311S	1864	YEV322S	1887	BNO677T	1897	DAR119T	1909	DAR131T
1857	YEV315S	1884	BNO674T						

7513-7569   Mercedes-Benz L608D   Dormobile   B20F   1986   Ex City Line, 1994-95

7513	D513FAE	7543w	D543FAE	7546w	D546FAE	7553w	D553FAE	7559w	D559FAE
7515	D515FAE	7544w	D544FAE	7547w	D547FAE	7557w	D557FAE	7565w	D565FAE
7533	D533FAE	7545w	D545FAE	7552w	D552FAE	7558	D558FAE	7569w	D569FAE
7542w	D542FAE								

Named vehicles: 500 *William Gammon*; 908 *Dylan Thomas*; 909 *Sir Harry Secombe*

Previous Registrations:

ACY178A	from new	IIL1828	B690BPU	MKH487A	from new
C312KTH	999BCY	IIL1829	B696BPU		

Livery: Green, red, yellow & white; white (National Express) 102/3/12-5, 131-3/5-7; silver, blue, black & red (Air Link) 104-11; red (Original Big Red Bus) 976/95

THOMAS COACHES

W G Thomas & partners, Bus Depot, Aberrhondda Road, Porth,
Rhondda Cynon Taff CF39 0AG
TD & KD Thomas, Maesgwyn, Blanche Street, Williamstown, Rhondda Cynon
Taff CF40 1NG

Depot : Aberrhondda Road, Porth,

YNA272M	Daimler Fleetline CRG6LXB	Northern Counties	H43/32F	1973	Ex Venture Travel, Cardiff, 1996
YNA299M	Daimler Fleetline CRG6LXB	Northern Counties	H43/32F	1973	Ex Venture Travel, Cardiff, 1996
YNA369M	Daimler Fleetline CRG6LXB	Northern Counties	H43/32F	1974	Ex Warrington, 1993
OEH604M	Bristol VRT/SL2/6LX	Eastern Coach Works	H43/31F	1974	Ex PMT, 1990
URN160R	Bristol VRT/SL3/6LXB	East Lancashire	H43/32F	1976	Ex Burnley & Pendle, 1989
URN163R	Bristol VRT/SL3/6LXB	East Lancashire	H43/32F	1976	Ex Burnley & Pendle, 1989
URN164R	Bristol VRT/SL3/6LXB	East Lancashire	H43/32F	1976	Ex Burnley & Pendle, 1989
NOC403R	Leyland Fleetline FE30ALR	MCW	H43/33F	1976	Ex Beeston, Hadleigh, 1994
NOC410R	Leyland Fleetline FE30ALR	MCW	H43/33F	1976	Ex Beeston, Hadleigh, 1994
NOC412R	Leyland Fleetline FE30ALR	MCW	H43/33F	1976	Ex West Midlands Travel, 1989
NOC493R	Leyland Fleetline FE30AGR	MCW	H43/33F	1977	Ex Atlas Bus, North Acton, 1994
OJD354R	Leyland Fleetline FE30ALR	Park Royal	H44/24D	1977	Ex Venture Travel, Cardiff, 1996
FDN583S	Leyland Fleetline FE30AGR	Roe	H43/33F	1976	Ex Dawlish Coaches, 1994
SDA509S	Leyland Fleetline FE30AGR	MCW	H43/33F	1977	Ex West Midlands Travel, 1989
SDA532S	Leyland Fleetline FE30AGR	MCW	H43/33F	1977	Ex West Midlands Travel, 1989
SDA631S	Leyland Fleetline FE30AGR	Park Royal	H43/33F	1977	Ex West Midlands Travel, 1989
SDA659S	Leyland Fleetline FE30AGR	Park Royal	H43/33F	1978	Ex Swanbrook, Cheltenham, 1995
AYG852S	Bristol VRT/SL3/6LXB	Eastern Coach Works	H43/31F	1978	Ex Rover, Bromsgrove, 1995
CWU151T	Leyland Fleetline FE30AGR	Roe	H43/33F	1978	Ex Yorkshire Rider, 1996

Thomas Coaches have had a substantial presence in South Wales for some years now. High specification coaches on Spanish/French shuttle work and double deck buses on school contracts have dominated although some minibuses and older coaches have also featured. A recent acquisition from Rhondda subsidiary, Parfitts, was this Duple Dominant IV-bodied Leyland Tiger. *John Jones*

As the competitive pressures built up for National Welsh at the end of the 1980s, opportunities arose for smaller operators to acquire school contracts which were less profitable for the former-NBC subsidiary. A number of double-decks were acquired in 1989 by Thomas including four East Lancashire-bodied Bristol VRs from Burnley and Pendle. *(Above)* One of the remaining three, URN160R, departs the depot at Porth. This was once part of the National Welsh complex in the town and was secured by Thomas before the death-throes of its neighbour forced the sale of the remainder of the site to Rhondda. *(Below)* Thomas did not have to go far to collect this purchase from the National Welsh receivers as BUH231V was Porth-based on its sale in 1992. *John Jones*

Thomas Coaches last non-Scania purchases for the coach fleet were a pair of Bova Futuras in 1994 and these are seen outside City Hall in Cardiff with L335DTG in the foreground. Most new purchases since 1979 have featured 330-339 in their registrations. *John Jones*

WMU43T	Ford R1014	Marshall	B55F	1979	Ex Trinant RFC, 1995
TDT1L	Bristol VRT/SL3/501	Eastern Coach Works	H43/31F	1980	Ex Brewers, 1994
BUH231V	Bristol VRT/SL3/501	Eastern Coach Works	H43/31F	1980	Ex National Welsh, 1992
FHO86W	Ford R1114	Plaxton Supreme IV	C53F	1980	Ex Rhondda, 1996
B804ETG	Leyland Tiger TRCTL11/3R	Duple Dominant IV	C57F	1984	Ex Parfitt's, 1995
B828ETG	Scania K112CRS	Berkhof Esprite 350	C53F	1985	Ex AJC, Leeds, 1995
PNK1M	Scania K112CRS	Plaxton Paramount 3500	C53F	1985	Ex Swallow, Bristol, 1994
G116CSJ	Mercedes-Benz 609D	Crystals	C24F	1990	Ex Fairline Mini Cs, Glasgow, 1995
G117CSJ	Mercedes-Benz 609D	Crystals	C24F	1990	Ex Fairline Mini Cs, Glasgow, 1995
H220GKK	Ford Transit VE6	Crystals	C16F	1991	
H818RWJ	Scania K113CRB	Plaxton Paramount 3500 III	C53F	1991	Ex Acorn, Bristol, 1994
J212XKY	Scania K93CRB	Plaxton Paramount 3200 III	C53F	1991	Ex Acorn, Bristol, 1994
J331TTX	Scania K113CRB	Berkhof Excellence 2000HL	C51FT	1992	
K330YDW	Scania K113TRB	Berkhof Excellence 3000HD	CH55/18CT	1992	
K331YDW	Mercedes-Benz 711D	Made-to-Measure	C24F	1992	
K332YDW	Bova FHD12.290	Bova Futura	C51FT	1993	
L681GKG	Ford Transit VE6	Ford	M14	1993	Ex private owner, 1995
L334DTG	Mercedes-Benz 711D	Dormobile Routemaker	C25F	1993	
L335DTG	Bova FHD12.290	Bova Futura	C53F	1994	
L336DTG	Bova FHD12.290	Bova Futura	C53F	1994	
L337DTG	Scania K113CRB	Berkhof Excellence 2000HL	C51FT	1994	
L338DTG	Scania K113TRA	Berkhof Excellence 3000HD	CH57/23DT	1994	
WGT1	Scania K113TRA	Berkhof Excellence 3000HD	CH57/23DT	1994	
M330JHB	Ford Transit VE6	Crystals Challenger	DP20F	1995	
YSU985	Scania K113TRA	Berkhof Excellence 3000HD	CH57/20DT	1995	
P	Scania K113TRA	Berkhof Excellence 3000HD	CH57/20DT	1996	

Previous Registrations:

B804ETG	B733ATG, JEP609	PNK1M	B470YHT, 578DAF, B470YHT
B828ETG	B413DHK, YSU985	TDT1L	BEP973V
L681GKG	L469UER, L1KDT	WGT1	From new

Livery: White, orange and blue; white and blue (Raillink) G116/7CSJ, K331YDW, M330JHB

TRC

TR Cole, Chwarteg, 4 Mace Lane, Treorchy, Rhondda Cynon Taff   CF42 6DS

Depot : Caemawr Ind Est, Treorchy and Mace Lane, Treorchy.

ULJ257J	Leyland Atlantean PDR1A/1	Alexander J	H43/31F	1971	Ex Yellow Buses, 1991
DLJ113L	Daimler Fleetline CRL6	Alexander J	H43/31F	1973	Ex Yellow Buses, 1992
XJF156S	Ford R1114	Plaxton Supreme III	C53F	1978	Ex Chalkwell, Sittingbourne, 1991
UTV220S	Leyland Fleetline FE30AGR	Northern Counties	H47/31D	1978	Ex Porthcawl Omnibus, 1996
JMB401T	Bristol VRT/SL3/501	Eastern Coach Works	H43/31F	1979	Ex Wilkins, Cymmer, 1992
FAX69V	Leyland Leopard PSU3F/5R	Plaxton Supreme IV	C53F	1980	Ex Humphreys, Pontypridd, 1993
FCY598W	Ford R1114	Duple Dominant	C53F	1980	Ex Smiths, Cymmer, 1991
A9TRC	Leyland Royal Tiger B50	Roe Doyen	C47FT	1984	Ex Dukes Travel, Edge End, 1993
TRC883G	Leyland Royal Tiger RTC	Plaxton Paramount 3500	C49FT	1985	Ex Nationwide, Lanark, 1989
A19TRC	Mercedes-Benz L608D	Reeve Burgess	C25F	1986	Ex USAF, 1995

Previous Registrations:

A9TRC	A101GAD, 3012WF, PAT189W	TRC883G	B137AAV
A19TRC	?		

Livery: Red and orange

Another beneficiary of the desire of National Welsh to rid itself of less-profitable contract work was Ralph Cole who started his business in 1989 but expanded quickly in 1991. In that year the long-established business, Smiths of Cymmer, was disbanded and four vehicles came to TRC. Ford/Duple Dominant FCY598W was one of these and it is seen, some years later in Aberdare. *John Jones*

One of the benefits of splitting the former Welsh Bus Handbook is the ability to include more operators. One most deserving of inclusion is Venture Travel of Cardiff. This business has tenuous links with the Morris Bros. empire who had a depot in Cardiff. They were taken over by Capitol of Cwmbran in 1984 but in 1987 the depot was purchased by CTC of Caerphilly along with several Capitol vehicles. This business was not entirely successful and two years later the depot and some vehicles were acquired by Venture Travel. Shown here are two of the double-deck fleet. *Above:* OJD354R, a DMS new to London and still retaining it's centre door, and *Below:* the most recent acquisition and partly repainted is ex Cardiff Bus WTG334T. *David Donati / John Jones*

VENTURE TRAVEL

AN Grisedale and RS Hart, Watford Road, Cardiff   CF2 7XL

1	GHV995N	Daimler Fleetline CRL6	Park Royal	H44/27D	1974	Ex CTC Cardiff, 1989
3	OJD462R	Leyland Fleetline FE30ALR	Park Royal	H44/24D	1977	Ex Wigan Bus Company, 1994
6	OJD375R	Leyland Fleetline FE30ALR	Park Royal	H44/24D	1977	Ex Wigan Bus Company, 1994
15	UDG206R	Leyland Leopard PSU3E/4R	Plaxton Supreme III	C53F	1977	Ex Geoff Willetts, Yorkley, 1994
12	THX273S	Leyland Fleetline FE30ALR	MCW	H44/24D	1977	Ex Wigan Bus Company, 1994
	WTG328T	Bristol VRT/SL3/6LXB	Alexander AL	H44/31F	1978	Ex Cardiff Bus, 1996
	WTG334T	Bristol VRT/SL3/6LXB	Alexander AL	H44/31F	1978	Ex Cardiff Bus, 1996
8	AEF819A	Leyland Leopard PSU3E/4R	Duple Dominant II Express	C49F	1979	Ex London Buses, 1990
	VOY180X	Leyland Tiger TRCTL11/2R	Plaxton Viewmaster IV Exp	C53F	1981	Ex British Airways, 1996
	VOY181X	Leyland Tiger TRCTL11/2R	Plaxton Viewmaster IV Exp	C53F	1981	Ex British Airways, 1995
11	NDW141X	Leyland Tiger TRCTL11/2R	Plaxton Supreme VI Express	C53F	1982	Ex Hill's of Tredegar, 1991
10	510EKH	Leyland Tiger TRCTL11/3R	Plaxton Paramount 3500	C52F	1983	Ex Arleen, Peasedown St John, 1994
13	JIL3254	Leyland Royal Tiger RT	Plaxton Paramount 3500 II	C50F	1985	Ex Online, Sutton, 1992
18	B348AMH	Leyland Royal Tiger RT	Van Hool Alizée	C53F	1985	Ex Tudor Cs, Colsterworth, 1994
14	JIL3253	Leyland Tiger TRCTL11/3RZ	Duple 340	C50FT	1986	Ex Parkers Cs, Newhall, 1992
	C489BFB	Ford Transit 190	Dormobile	B16F	1986	Ex Coombs, Weston-s-Mare, 1995
	E129RDW	MCW MetroRider MF150/31	MCW	DP23F	1987	Ex Cardiff Bus, 1996
	G584RNC	Peugeot-Talbot Express	Made-to-Measure	M14	1989	Ex Jennings, Bude, 1995

Previous Registrations:

510EKH	JNM758Y	JIL3253	C518WBF	UDG206R	SDD139R, 2464FH
AEF819A	OMA508V	JIL3254	C398DML		

Livery: Green and gold or green and white.

Another former Cardiff Bus acquisition in 1996 was this MCW MetroRider, E129RDW. This, in common with other recent arrivals, has not received a fleet number and that system is generally in abeyance. Of historical note is that the depot is adjacent to the former Cardiff tram, trolleybus and bus depot at Roath which has been re-developed as can be seen behind the subject of the photograph. *John Jones*

WATERHALL COACHES

R H John, Waterhall House, Waterhall Road, Kenfig Hill, Bridgend   CF33 6HD

JKE102L	Leyland Leopard PSU3E/4R	Duple Dominant	C44F	1973	Ex Sussex Police, 1987
JKE103L	Leyland Leopard PSU3E/4R	Duple Dominant	C44F	1973	Ex Sussex Police, 1987
KEH878N	Leyland Leopard PSU3E/4R	Plaxton Elite III	C57F	1975	Ex Kenfig Motors, Pontycymmer, 1993
MAU141P	Bristol VRT/SL3/6LX	Eastern Coach Works	H39/31F	1976	Ex Stephenson, Rochford, 1994
URN161R	Bristol VRT/SL3/6LXB	East Lancashire	H43/32F	1976	Ex Village, Garston, 1994
URN162R	Bristol VRT/SL3/6LXB	East Lancashire	H43/32F	1976	Ex Village, Garston, 1994
VVA7T	Ford R1114	Plaxton Supreme IV	C53F	1979	Ex Mansel David, Pontycymmer, 1995
APM107T	AEC Reliance 6U2R	Plaxton Supreme IV Express	C49F	1979	Ex T&J Coaches, Orprington, 1995
ODJ583W	Volvo B58-61	Duple Dominant II	C53F	1981	Ex Shearings, 1988
E517PWR	Volkswagen LT55	Optare City Pacer	B25F	1987	Ex County, 1992

Previous Registrations:

KEH878N	HWU61N, 488BDN	VVA7T	DWK420T

Livery: White and two-tone green

Waterhall Coaches acquired three double decks in 1994 for newly-won Mid Glamorgan schools contracts. Many of these contracts are being re-tendered by the new County Borough of Bridgend over the summer of 1996 so changes here, as well as with other operators, can be expected. Two of the three Bristol VRs acquired have East Lancashire bodywork as demonstrated here by URN161R. *John Jones*

The South Wales Bus Handbook

WATTS

R A Watts, Old Post Garage, Bonvilston, Vale of Glamorgan   CF5 6TQ

Depots : Old Post Garage, Bonvilston and Pentre Farm, Llantrithyd

RUJ350R	Ford R1114	Plaxton Supreme III	C53F	1977	Ex Venture Travel, Cardiff, 1990
BDM207S	Ford R1114	Caetano Estoril	C53F	1977	Ex CK, Cardiff, 1982
XDG57S	Ford R1014	Plaxton Supreme III	C45F	1978	Ex Stevens, Warmley, 1981
ERW265T	Ford R1114	Duple Dominant II Express	C53F	1978	Ex Bebb, Llantwit Fardre, 1987
CWG692V	Leyland Atlantean AN68A/1R	Alexander AL	H45/29D	1979	Ex Camm, Nottingham, 1993
DKG321V	Ford R1014	Plaxton Supreme IV	C53F	1979	Ex Warner Fairfax, Tewkesbury, 1984
YPC559Y	Ford R1114	Duple Dominant IV	C53F	1982	Ex Evans, Tregaron, 1992
FUA394Y	Volvo B10M-61	Plaxton Paramount 3200	C53F	1983	Ex Woodstones, Kidderminster, 1989
THL296Y	Volvo B10M-61	Duple Caribbean	C50F	1983	Ex Shirley, Walsall, 1989
B568AHD	DAF SB2300DHTD585	Plaxton Paramount 3200	C53F	1985	Ex Hurst & Leak, Goose Green, 1992
C280VFP	DAF MB200DKFL600	Plaxton Paramount 3200	C53F	1986	Ex Bland, Stamford, 1990
E53MMT	Leyland Tiger TRCL10/3RZ	Duple 340	C53FT	1987	Ex Classic, Annfield Plain, 1992
E42HLP	Mercedes-Benz 609D	Reeve Burgess Beaver	C19F	1988	Ex EMMS, Nantgarw, 1993
E380MPX	Mercedes-Benz 811D	Robin Hood	C29F	1988	Ex Wings, Uxbridge, 1991
F598BTG	Leyland Tiger TRCL10/3ARZM	Plaxton Paramount 3500 III	C51FT	1989	Ex Hills of Tredegar, 1992
F149TEU	Mercedes-Benz 609D	Made-to-Measure	C24F	1989	
G54RTO	Volvo B10M-60	Duple 340	C55F	1990	Ex Turner, Bristol, 1996
G55RTO	Volvo B10M-60	Duple 340	C55F	1990	Ex Turner, Bristol, 1996
H185EJF	MAN 10-180	Caetano Algarve II	C35F	1991	

Livery: Fawn, red and gold

Roly Watts commenced in the early 1960s from a service station at Bonvilston moving to a similar site further along the A48 in the mid 1980s. An all-lightweight fleet was operated until 1989 when the first Volvo arrived since when a variety of vehicles has been operated. The front line fleet includes B568AHD a DAF with Plaxton Paramount I body (rebuilt with mark III front) and they sport an attractive livery, always well presented. *John Jones*

WELSH DRAGON

A B Smith, 436 Corporation Road, Newport   NP9 0GA

Depot : Telford Street, Newport

868NHT	Bristol Lodekka FS6G	Eastern Coach Works	CO33/27R	1961	Ex Weston Carnival Club, 1988
AFE171A	Bristol Lodekka FS6B	Eastern Coach Works	CO33/27R	1962	Ex RoadCar, 1990
BOD25C	Bristol Lodekka FLF6B	Eastern Coach Works	H38/32F	1965	Ex Western National, 1978
XWU339S	Bristol VRT/SL3/6LXB	Eastern Coach Works	H43/31F	1977	Ex Teeside, 1994
ODV405W	AEC Reliance 6U2R	Duple Dominant II Express	C53F	1981	Ex Metrobus, Orpington, 1995
TDL483X	Leyland Leopard PSU3G/4R	Eastern Coach Works	C51F	1982	Ex Southern Vectis, 1991
PVV318	Bova EL26/581	Bova Europa	C52F	1983	Ex Sharon Coaches, Addlestone, 1989
E131SNY	MCW MetroRider MF150/53	MCW	DP23F	1988	Ex Cardiff Bus, 1996

Previous Registrations:

868NHT	from new	PVV318	JRO612Y
AFE171A	XPM42	TDL483X	RDL309X, VDL263

The Welsh Dragon fleet has always been an intriguing one with variety and interest at all times. Had a Bristol LH and one LHS not been sold earlier this year it may have been even more varied. Of the Lodekkas owned only the FS6G is currently in use though others may enter service again. Bova Futura PVV318 is seen in this view adjacent to Newport bus station. *John Jones*

WHEADON'S GREYHOUND COACHES

E K Wheadon, Station Terrace, Cowbridge Road West, Ely Bridge, Cardiff   CF5 4AA

IIL2565	Volvo B58-56	Plaxton P'mount 3200(1985)	C40F	1975	Ex Greyhound, Cardiff, 1995
JRT710N	Bedford YRT	Plaxton Derwent	B55F	1975	Ex Greyhound, Cardiff, 1995
OAX615R	Bedford VAS5	Plaxton Supreme III	C29F	1976	Ex Greyhound, Cardiff, 1995
BDN20R	Bedford YMT	Plaxton Supreme III	C53F	1977	Ex Greyhound, Cardiff, 1995
DNK428T	Bedford YMT	Duple Dominant II	C53F	1979	Ex Greyhound, Cardiff, 1995
CRM114T	Bedford YMT	Duple Dominant II	C53F	1979	Ex Greyhound, Cardiff, 1995
HVC8V	Bedford YMT	Plaxton Supreme IV	C53F	1979	Ex Greyhound, Cardiff, 1995
KPP615V	Ford Transit 160	Tricentrol	M12	1980	Ex Greyhound, Cardiff, 1995
MMJ549V	Bedford YMT	Duple Dominant II	C53F	1980	Ex Greyhound, Cardiff, 1995
PPC335W	Bedford YMT	Duple Dominant II	C53F	1980	Ex Greyhound, Cardiff, 1995
JMR858W	Bedford YNT	Plaxton Supreme IV Express	C53F	1981	Ex Greyhound, Cardiff, 1995
OJI5267	Bedford YNT	Duple Dominant III	C53F	1982	Ex Greyhound, Cardiff, 1995
A59NPP	Mercedes-Benz L608D	Reeve Burgess	C19F	1984	Ex Scott, Marley Hill, 1989
IIL2566	Bedford YNT	Plaxton Paramount 3200	C53F	1985	Ex Greyhound, Cardiff, 1995
C439SJU	Ford Transit	Robin Hood	B16F	1985	Ex Tellings-Golden Miller, 1991
C448SJU	Ford Transit	Robin Hood	B16F	1985	Ex Tellings-Golden Miller, 1991
D384KND	Ford Transit	Mellor	M4L	1985	Ex Kent CC, 1991
YNY58	Freight Rover Sherpa	Freight Rover	M16	1989	Ex Smart minicoaches, Penarth, 1994
F248VBX	Renault Trafic	Holdsworth	M9	1989	Ex private owner, 1991
L58YJF	Toyota Coaster HZB50R	Caetano Optimo III	C21F	1993	
L697CNR	Toyota Coaster HZB50R	Caetano Optimo III	C21F	1994	
M485HBC	MAN 11.190	Caetano Algarve II	C35F	1994	
N251NNR	Toyota Coaster HZB50R	Caetano Optimo III	C21F	1996	
N253NNR	Toyota Coaster HZB50R	Caetano Optimo III	C21F	1995	
N254NNR	Toyota Coaster HZB50R	Caetano Optimo III	C21F	1995	

Previous Registrations:

IIL2565	GYT145N, B188XJD	OJI5267	BRO585X
IIL2566	B249AMG, OJI9476	PPC335W	WWM843W, 65KD42
JMR858W	GMW781W, YWV424	YNY58	??

Livery: White, blue and grey

Wheadon's Greyhound Coaches came about as a result of the takeover of Greyhound Coaches, established by Thomas James in 1967, by Wheadons started by Ernie Wheadon in 1982. Both concerns relied heavily on mini and midi coaches in their early years although the Greyhound fleet almost wholly comprised full size vehicles when they were acquired. Wheadon's, in contrast, specialised in the smaller end of the market albeit with high quality work. The only bus in the fleet remains this Plaxton Derwent-bodied Bedford JRT710N. *John Jones*

Wherever Duples Dominant III bodywork is described there is inevitably a reference to the famous Greyhound coaches of the United States (see page 17). This picture of OJI5267 (above) demonstrates the nearest one is likely to get to realising the myth. This Bedford YNT shows the Greyhound white and blue scheme compared with (below) M485HBC which carries Wheadons white, blue and grey on its Caetano Algarve II body. In due course the latter scheme will prevail. *John Jones*

WHITE LION

B Hillman, Crown Garage, Merthyr Road, Ashvale,
Tredegar, Blaenau Gwent NP2 3RX

XVJ771	Volvo B58-56	Plaxton Supreme III Express C53F		1976	Ex Noble, Fraserburgh, 1988
TWC298	Volvo B58-56	Plaxton Supreme III	C46F	1978	Ex The Wright Company, Wrexham, 1992
JIL2432	Volvo B58-56	Plaxton Supreme III	C53F	1978	Ex Dorking Coaches, 1994
TXI8759	Volvo B58-61	Plaxton Supreme IV	C53F	1979	Ex Thomas of Barry, 1992
NEU430	Volvo B58-56	Plaxton Supreme IV Express C53F		1981	Ex The Wright Company, Wrexham, 1992
NIW5983	Volvo B10M-61	Plaxton Supreme V	C53F	1982	Ex Tillingbourne, Cranleigh, 1995
JIL2433	Volvo B10M-61	Plaxton Supreme V	C53F	1982	Ex Dorking Coaches, 1993
KXI366	Volvo B10M-61	Plaxton Paramount 3500	C49F	1983	Ex Epsom Coaches, 1992
GIL2409	Volvo B10M-61	Plaxton Paramount 3500	C40FT	1983	Ex Paul S Winson, Loughborough, 1991
KXI169	Volvo B10M-61	Plaxton Paramount 3200 II	C57F	1985	Ex Evans, New Tredegar, 1995
KXI318	Volvo B10M-61	Plaxton Paramount 3500 III	C49FT	1988	Ex Bailey, Biddisham, 1995
E305OMG	Volvo B10M-61	Plaxton Paramount 3500 III	C49F	1988	Ex Limebourne, Battersea, 1995

Previous Registrations:

GIL2409	A772HKA, FDJ7S	KXI318	E326UUB	TWC298	DMA367S
JIL2432	XEH3S, 9039RU, UTS791S	KXI366	NGT1Y	TXI8759	SDR436T
JIL2433	LWN126X	NEU430	PJU261W	XVJ771	RNP955P
KXI169	B664OFP	NIW5983	LWN125X		

Livery: Grey and red

Bernard Hillman started White Lion Minibuses in 1983 and adopted a dual grey and red livery and logo which echoes that latterly employed by R I Davies. That operator finally disappeared into the Hills of Tredegar business in 1978 but retained a degree of local goodwill. Minibuses only were operated until 1986 since when an all-Volvo/Plaxton fleet has been amassed. The operator is particularly noted for its coachbuilding activities and the high standard of presentation of the older vehicles is testament to thorough preparation before entering service often involving new fronts and repanelling. Cherished registrations such as NEU430 seen here in Cardiff, are used extensively.
John Jones

WILKINS TRAVEL

Wilkins Bros (Cymmer) Ltd, Eastern Avenue, Croeserw, Cymmer,
Neath & Port Talbot SA13 3PB

Depots : Il Heol Ty Gwyn, Tyle Teg, Maesteg and Johns Terrace, Tonmawr.

MCY85G	AEC Reliance 6U3ZR	Duple Dominant II(1981)	C53F	1969	Ex Tenby Bus & Coach, 1991
HTG557K	Leyland Leopard PSU3B/4R	Plaxton Elite III Express	C53F	1972	Ex Creamline, Tonmawr, 1987
AEA485M	Leyland Leopard PSU3B/4R	Plaxton Elite III Express	C53F	1974	Ex Sargent, Cardiff, 1991
OWN250R	Bedford YMT	Plaxton Derwent	B55F	1977	Ex Creamline, Tonmawr, 1987
PSD521R	Leyland Leopard PSU5A/4R	Plaxton Supreme III	C57F	1977	Ex Castell Coaches, Trethomas, 1995
REG480R	Leyland Leopard PSU3C/4R	Plaxton Supreme III Express	C53F	1977	Ex Gwendraeth Valley, Drefach, 1995
SVO782R	AEC Reliance 6U2R	Plaxton Supreme III	C53F	1977	Ex Kettlewell, Retford, 1992
ROU348S	Leyland Leopard PSU3E/4R	Plaxton Supreme III Express	C49F	1978	Ex Cheltenham & Gloucester, 1987
ATH179T	AEC Reliance 6U3ZR	Duple Dominant II	C53F	1979	Ex Tenby Bus & Coach, 1991
MYD215V	Bedford YMT	Plaxton Supreme IV	C53F	1980	Ex Lewis Coaches, Aberdare, 1994
EHW288W	Ford R1114	Duple Dominant II	C53F	1981	Ex Turner, Bristol, 1986
VBM716W	DAF MB200DKTL600	Plaxton Supreme IV	C53F	1981	Ex Gregory, Blaencwm, 1993
SND303X	Leyland Leopard PSU5C/4R	Plaxton Supreme V	C53F	1981	Ex Cheltenham & Gloucester, 1987
KEC976X	Bedford YNT	Plaxton Supreme V	C53F	1982	Ex Silver Badge, Windermere, 1983
RDT121X	Leyland Tiger TRCTL11/3R	Duple Dominant IV	C53F	1982	Ex Pullman, Crofty, 1994
OHV190Y	Ford R1114	Wadham Stringer Vanguard	B32F	1982	Ex LB Southwark, 1994
OHV193Y	Ford R1114	Wadham Stringer Vanguard	B32F	1982	Ex LB Southwark, 1994
OHV209Y	Ford R1114	Wadham Stringer Vanguard	B32F	1982	Ex LB Southwark, 1994
KIW3766	DAF MB200DKFL600	LAG Galaxy	C49FT	1986	
C768MVH	DAF MB230DKFL615	Duple 340	C57F	1986	Ex Harris, Catshill, 1991
C109HKG	Ford Transit	Robin Hood	B16F	1986	Ex Rhondda, 1992
C110HKG	Ford Transit	Robin Hood	B16F	1986	Ex Rhondda, 1992
551FVW	DAF MB230DKFL615	Duple 340	C53FT	1986	Ex Castell Coaches, Trethomas, 1995
E110RAX	Freight Rover Sherpa	Carlyle Citybus 2	B20F	1987	Ex Rhondda, 1992
OIJ864	Leyland Royal Tiger RTC	Leyland Doyen	C53F	1988	Ex West Riding, 1989
E51TYG	Leyland Royal Tiger RTC	Leyland Doyen	C53F	1988	Ex West Riding, 1989
F164JOD	DAF SB3000DKV601	Caetano Algarve	C49FT	1988	Ex Garratt, Newton Abbot, 1994
G991OKJ	DAF MB230LT615	Caetano Algarve	C53F	1989	Ex The King's Ferry, 1993

Previous Registrations:

551FVW	D756KKG	KIW3766	B73BCY	OIJ864	E50TYG
ATH179T	AHE996T, KIW3766	MCY85G	LWM475G, OIJ864		

Livery: Cream, tan and brown; white, blue and grey E51YTG, F164JOD; white (Majestic Holidays) OIJ864

Wilkins Travel is based at Cymmer in the Afan Valley although its depots are the former Creamline garage at Tonmawr and another in the Llynfi Valley at Maesteg. Seen in Cymmer however is ROU348S an ex Cheltenham & Gloucester Leyland Leopard. *John Jones*

Contract vehicles feature heavily in the Wilkins fleet and these generally carry the cream, tan and brown livery. Front line coaches however either carry that scheme or a white, blue and grey one based on the Ridings Travel livery in which the two Royal Tigers arrived in 1989. Here *(above)* in the general scheme is C768MVH while similarly attired *(below)* is G991OKJ both are similar mid-engined DAFs but with considerably differing bodies. *John Jones*

Index to Vehicles

93FYB	Ken Hopkins	A514VKG	Cardiff Bus	AWN810V	Brewers	BNO677T	S W T
99KMH	Ken Hopkins	A515VKG	Cardiff Bus	AWN812V	Brewers	BOD25C	Welsh Dragon
210HKT	Edwards Coaches	A516VKG	Cardiff Bus	AWN813V	S W T	BPA342K	Edwards Coaches
219LUO	Edwards Coaches	A517VKG	Cardiff Bus	AWN815V	S W T	BPT903S	Red & White
278TNY	Brewers	A518VKG	Cardiff Bus	AYG852S	Thomas Coaches	BTU636S	Rees Travel
300CUH	Brewers	A519VKG	Cardiff Bus	AYR323T	Nelson's Travel	BUH211V	Red & White
431DWN	Brian Issac	A539XUH	Phil Anslow Travel	AYR349T	Shamrock	BUH212V	Red & White
474CUH	Cyril Evans	A541HAC	Red & White	B26ADW	Rhondda	BUH214V	Red & White
510EKH	Venture Travel	A548HAC	Red & White	B27ADW	Rhondda	BUH231V	Thomas Coaches
540CCY	Brian Issac	A549HAC	Red & White	B208TBU	Ken Hopkins	BUH232V	Red & White
551FVW	Wilkins Travel	A616WEP	Hawkes	B219YUH	Newport	BUH237V	Red & White
561AH	Ken Hopkins	A658KUM	Brewers	B220YUH	Newport	BUH238V	Morris Travel
581BXP	Diamond Glantawe	A670KUM	Brewers	B221OJU	Edwards Coaches	BVA784V	Phil Anslow Travel
680XAE	Shamrock	A691OHJ	Brewers	B221WEU	Brewers	BWE210T	Brian Issac
723CTH	Hawkes	A693OHJ	Brewers	B221YUH	Newport	BYW383V	Rhondda
769DAF	Rees Travel	A695OHJ	Brewers	B222YUH	Newport	BYW393V	Rhondda
794YKM	Diamond Glantawe	A707YKG	Express	B223YUH	Newport	BYW397V	Rhondda
868NHT	Welsh Dragon	A724FRM	Express	B224YUH	Newport	C27ETG	Newport
898FCY	Hawkes	AAL423A	Porthcawl Omnibus	B225YUH	Newport	C28ETG	Newport
948RJO	Brewers	AAL516A	Red & White	B226YUH	Newport	C29ETG	Newport
978HHT	Edwards Coaches	AAL518A	Red & White	B292RJF	Rees Travel	C30ETG	Newport
2039NU	Harris	AAL538A	Red & White	B320RJF	Rees Travel	C31ETG	Newport
2375NU	Harris	AAL544A	Red & White	B348AMH	Venture Travel	C32ETG	Newport
8845EL	Len Hopkins	AAL575A	Red & White	B371PLK	Perry's Supreme	C33ETG	Newport
A9TRC	T R C	AAL587A	Rhondda	B444OCC	Hawthorn	C34ETG	Newport
A13RBL	Rhondda	AAL622A	Rhondda	B551ATX	Cardiff Bus	C41GKG	I B T
A14RBL	Rhondda	AAX450A	Red & White	B552ATX	Cardiff Bus	C42GKG	I B T
A15RBL	Rhondda	AAX451A	Red & White	B553ATX	Cardiff Bus	C43GKG	I B T
A17RBL	Rhondda	AAX465A	Red & White	B554ATX	Cardiff Bus	C101DWR	Capitol Coaches
A19RBL	Rhondda	AAX466A	Red & White	B555ATX	Cardiff Bus	C109HKG	Wilkins Travel
A19TRC	T R C	AAX488A	Red & White	B556ATX	Cardiff Bus	C110HKG	Wilkins Travel
A20RBL	Rhondda	AAX489A	Red & White	B557ATX	Cardiff Bus	C111DWR	Capitol Coaches
A59NPP	Wheadon's G'hound	AAX515A	Red & White	B558ATX	Cardiff Bus	C113DWR	Capitol Coaches
A63OJX	Hawthorn	AAX516A	Red & White	B559ATX	Cardiff Bus	C114DWR	Capitol Coaches
A106YEP	Pullman Coaches	AAX529A	Red & White	B568AHD	Watts	C116DWR	Capitol Coaches
A151HLV	Cardiff Bus	ACY50D	Diamond Glantawe	B654ETG	Gavenny Bus	C123DWR	Capitol Coaches
A152HLV	Cardiff Bus	ACY51D	Diamond Glantawe	B804ETG	Thomas Coaches	C201HTH	Brewers
A154HLV	Cardiff Bus	ACY62D	Diamond Glantawe	B828ETG	Thomas Coaches	C202HTH	Brewers
A156HLV	Cardiff Bus	ACY178A	S W T	B905DHB	Brewers	C203HTH	Brewers
A158HLV	Cardiff Bus	AEA485M	Wilkins Travel	B906DHB	Brewers	C204HTH	Brewers
A159HLV	Cardiff Bus	AEF32Y	Edwards Coaches	B912AAX	Capitol Coaches	C205HTH	Brewers
A160HLV	Cardiff Bus	AEF819A	Venture Travel	B913AAX	Capitol Coaches	C206HTH	Brewers
A161HLV	Cardiff Bus	AET185T	Red & White	B973OSB	Rhondda	C207HTH	Brewers
A162HLV	Cardiff Bus	AEX402X	Hawthorn	BCJ700L	Hawkes	C208HTH	Brewers
A163HLV	Cardiff Bus	AFE171A	Welsh Dragon	BCK942V	C & E Travel	C209HJN	Brewers
A227MDD	Red & White	AKG197A	Red & White	BCY383V	Express	C209HTH	Brewers
A270HAY	Phillips	AKG214A	Red & White	BDM207S	Watts	C210HTH	Brewers
A298SPS	Perry's Supreme	AKG271A	Red & White	BDN20R	Wheadon's G'hound	C211HTH	Brewers
A310UEP	Brian Işsac	AKG296A	Red & White	BEP971V	Brewers	C212HTH	Brewers
A390VBO	Rees Travel	AKK174T	G M	BEP972V	Brewers	C213HTH	Brewers
A428VNY	Cardiff Bus	ANJ305T	Brian Issac	BEP974V	Brewers	C214HTH	Brewers
A429VNY	Cardiff Bus	ANJ312T	Brian Issac	BEP975V	S W T	C215HTH	S W T
A430VNY	Cardiff Bus	ANJ314T	Brian Issac	BEP976V	S W T	C221HJN	Brewers
A431VNY	Cardiff Bus	ANY587T	Hawkes	BEP977V	Brewers	C262AWR	Cyril Evans
A432VNY	Cardiff Bus	APM107T	Waterhall	BEP980V	S W T	C280VFP	Watts
A433VNY	Cardiff Bus	APM116T	Mansell David	BEP981V	Brewers	C285EHU	Hawkes
A434VNY	Cardiff Bus	ATH179T	Wilkins Travel	BEP982V	Brewers	C312KTH	S W T
A435VNY	Cardiff Bus	ATH352V	Merlyn's	BEP984V	S W T	C327UFP	Shamrock
A436VNY	Cardiff Bus	AUJ706T	Ken Hopkins	BEP985V	Brewers	C328UFP	Shamrock
A447PFO	Shamrock	AUJ711T	Brian Issac	BEP986V	Brewers	C330MLG	Shamrock
A500WGF	Hawthorn	AUJ722T	Castell Coaches	BFP260Y	Phillips	C336UFP	Len Hopkins
A511VKG	Cardiff Bus	AVK163V	Red & White	BFX745T	Hawthorn	C349RPE	Porthcawl Omnibus
A512VKG	Cardiff Bus	AVK166V	Red & White	BKH301X	Hawthorn	C350RPE	Porthcawl Omnibus
A513VKG	Cardiff Bus	AVK173V	Red & White	BNO674T	S W T	C406WCJ	Martin

Capitol have several Volvo B10M coaches in the fleet that were new to Wallace Arnold, the Yorkshire tour operator. The number of this chassis now totals thirteen, all but four Duple 340s being bodied by Plaxton now part of the Henly Group. One of the Scarborough-built products, H611UWR is seen unloading adjacent to Cardiff's New Theatre. *John Jones*

Reg	Operator	Reg	Operator	Reg	Operator	Reg	Operator
C439SJU	Wheadon's G'hound	CBV790S	Glyn Williams	D186PWN	Harris	D247LCY	S W T
C448SJU	Wheadon's G'hound	CFX308T	Howells Coaches	D212MBO	Gavenny Bus	D248LCY	S W T
C450WFO	Ken Hopkins	CFX318T	Nelson's Travel	D213LWX	Capitol Coaches	D249LCY	S W T
C478BHY	Brewers	CNR77T	Ken Hopkins	D214LWX	Capitol Coaches	D250LCY	S W T
C480BHY	Brewers	CRM114T	Wheadon's G'hound	D215LWX	Capitol Coaches	D251LCY	S W T
C481BHY	Brewers	CTX382V	Cardiff Bus	D216LWX	Capitol Coaches	D252LCY	S W T
C488JCY	Martin	CTX384V	Cardiff Bus	D217LCY	Brewers	D253LCY	S W T
C489BFB	Venture Travel	CTX386V	Cardiff Bus	D219LCY	Brewers	D257PEP	Harris
C499FAX	Henley's	CTX388V	Cardiff Bus	D220LCY	S W T	D300XCX	Harris
C560GWO	Cardiff Bus	CTX391V	Cardiff Bus	D221LCY	S W T	D317UTU	Henley's
C561GWO	Cardiff Bus	CTX392V	Cardiff Bus	D222LCY	S W T	D362SDM	Shamrock
C562GWO	Cardiff Bus	CTX393V	Cardiff Bus	D223LCY	S W T	D363SDM	Shamrock
C563GWO	Cardiff Bus	CTX394V	Cardiff Bus	D224LCY	S W T	D384KND	Wheadon's G'hound
C564GWO	Cardiff Bus	CTX395V	Cardiff Bus	D225LCY	S W T	D402OWN	Brian Issac
C565GWO	Cardiff Bus	CTX396V	Cardiff Bus	D226LCY	S W T	D403OWN	Brian Issac
C566GWO	Cardiff Bus	CUP759W	Coastal Continental	D227LCY	S W T	D404OWN	Brian Issac
C567GWO	Cardiff Bus	CWG692V	Watts	D228LCY	S W T	D405NUH	I B T
C598HTX	Edwards Coaches	CWG760V	Cardiff Bluebird	D229LCY	S W T	D406NUH	I B T
C644KDS	Hawkes	CWU142T	Brian Issac	D230LCY	S W T	D407NUH	Pullman Coaches
C684WKS	Burrows	CWU145T	Brian Issac	D232LCY	S W T	D408NUH	I B T
C722JJO	Harris	CWU147T	Brian Issac	D233LCY	S W T	D412NNA	Cardiff Bluebird
C723JJO	Harris	CWU151T	Thomas Coaches	D233PWN	Diamond Glantawe	D418FEH	Harris
C768MVH	Wilkins Travel	CYJ492Y	Red & White	D234LCY	S W T	D420NNA	Cardiff Bluebird
C901FCY	S W T	CYJ493Y	Red & White	D235LCY	S W T	D469PON	Cardiff Bluebird
C902FCY	S W T	D30VEY	Castell Coaches	D236LCY	S W T	D472PON	Rhondda
C902HWF	Red & White	D31MWN	S W T	D237LCY	S W T	D473PON	Rhondda
C903FCY	S W T	D44MBO	I B T	D238LCY	S W T	D477PON	Cardiff Bluebird
C904FCY	S W T	D46MBO	I B T	D239LCY	S W T	D478PON	Newport
C905FCY	S W T	D65OKG	Llynfi Coaches	D240LCY	S W T	D479PON	Rhondda
C906FCY	S W T	D73TLV	Brian Issac	D241LCY	S W T	D481PON	Rhondda
C907FCY	S W T	D108CKV	Howells Coaches	D242LCY	S W T	D513FAE	S W T
C974GCV	Brewers	D109NDW	Red & White	D243LCY	S W T	D514FAE	S W T
C975GCV	Brewers	D132NUS	Brian Issac	D244LCY	S W T	D515FAE	S W T
C976GCV	Brewers	D132WCC	Howells Coaches	D244VNL	John's Travel	D517FAE	Brewers
C977GCV	Brewers	D151NON	Harris	D245LCY	S W T	D520FAE	Brewers
CAC770T	Edwards Coaches	D182LAX	Phil Anslow Travel	D246LCY	S W T	D526FAE	Brewers

Reg	Operator	Reg	Operator	Reg	Operator	Reg	Operator
D527FAE	Brewers	DWA707V	Arthur Thomas	E381TEP	Hawkes	F94KDS	I B T
D533FAE	S W T	DWJ563V	Cardiff Bluebird	E517PWR	Waterhall	F99CEP	S W T
D540RCK	Red & White	DWY662T	Porthcawl Omnibus	E631KYW	Cardiff Bluebird	F99UNV	Rees Travel
D542FAE	S W T	E37UBO	Newport	E632KYW	Cardiff Bluebird	F100CEP	S W T
D543FAE	S W T	E38UBO	Newport	E634KYW	Cardiff Bluebird	F101YWO	Rhondda
D544FAE	S W T	E42HLP	Watts	E639KYW	Cardiff Bluebird	F104YWO	Rhondda
D544RCK	Red & White	E51TYG	Wilkins Travel	E647TOJ	Diamond Glantawe	F105YWO	Rhondda
D545FAE	S W T	E53MMT	Watts	E657VHF	C & E Travel	F106YWO	Rhondda
D546FAE	S W T	E62WDT	Rhondda	E717MFS	Perry's Supreme	F107YWO	Rhondda
D547FAE	S W T	E63WDT	Rhondda	E753NGA	Ferris Holidays	F108YWO	Rhondda
D552FAE	S W T	E97OUH	Hawkes	E807FRY	Shamrock	F109YWO	Rhondda
D553FAE	S W T	E110RAX	Wilkins Travel	E811UDT	Cardiff Bluebird	F110YWO	Rhondda
D557FAE	S W T	E113RBO	Red & White	E812UDT	Cardiff Bluebird	F112AHB	Shamrock
D558FAE	S W T	E114SDW	Red & White	E814XHS	Glyn Williams	F112YWO	Rhondda
D559FAE	S W T	E115SDW	Red & White	E823WWF	Llynfi Coaches	F113AHB	Shamrock
D565FAE	S W T	E126AAL	John's Travel	E837BTN	Cardiff Bluebird	F114YWO	Rhondda
D568EWS	Martin	E128KYW	Rhondda	E918AFM	Shamrock	F116EKO	Cardiff Bluebird
D569FAE	S W T	E129RDW	Venture Travel	E940THB	Hawkes	F116YWO	Rhondda
D574EWS	Gavenny Bus	E131SNY	Welsh Dragon	E947LAE	Phil Anslow Travel	F117YWO	Rhondda
D583EWS	Gavenny Bus	E133SNY	Harris	E948LAE	Phil Anslow Travel	F125YVP	Rhondda
D600KTX	Perry's Supreme	E136SNY	Harris	E949LAE	Phil Anslow Travel	F127AEL	Castell Coaches
D708TWM	Cardiff Bluebird	E138KYW	Cardiff Bluebird	E950LAE	Phil Anslow Travel	F128AEL	Castell Coaches
D709TWM	Cardiff Bluebird	E142TBO	Cardiff Bus	E953LAE	Phil Anslow Travel	F130YVP	Harris
D739JUB	John's Travel	E185UKG	Henley's	E954LAE	Phil Anslow Travel	F131YVP	Harris
D820SGB	Porthcawl Omnibus	E203PWY	Brewers	E955LAE	Phil Anslow Travel	F134DEP	S W T
D861NVS	Cardiff Bluebird	E204PWY	Brewers	E956LAE	Phil Anslow Travel	F135DEP	S W T
D862NVS	Cardiff Bluebird	E206BOD	S W T	E957LAE	Phil Anslow Travel	F149TEU	Watts
D864NVS	Cardiff Bluebird	E250MHX	C & E Travel	E958LAE	Phil Anslow Travel	F150AWO	Cardiff Bus
D865NVS	Cardiff Bluebird	E253ACC	Brian Issac	E961PME	Silverline	F150TRY	Harris
D875LWR	Harris	E261REP	Cardiff Bluebird	E962JBC	C & E Travel	F151AWO	Cardiff Bus
D879UFJ	Shamrock	E262REP	Cardiff Bluebird	E978DGS	Harris	F152AWO	Cardiff Bus
D889MWR	I B T	E267BRG	John's Travel	EAE684W	Phillips	F153AWO	Cardiff Bus
D896NUA	Silverline	E269REP	Cardiff Bluebird	ECA160S	Express	F154AWO	Cardiff Bus
D901MWR	Silverline	E270REP	Cardiff Bluebird	ECJ964W	Martin	F155AWO	Cardiff Bus
D911HOU	Phil Anslow Travel	E272BRG	John's Travel	ECY988V	Brewers	F156AWO	Cardiff Bus
D912HOU	Phil Anslow Travel	E279TTH	S W T	ECY989V	S W T	F157AWO	Cardiff Bus
D913HOU	Phil Anslow Travel	E280TTH	S W T	ECY991V	S W T	F158AWO	Cardiff Bus
D917HOU	Phil Anslow Travel	E281TTH	S W T	EEP395V	Ken Hopkins	F159AWO	Cardiff Bus
D918HOU	Phil Anslow Travel	E282TTH	S W T	EEU359	Cyril Evans	F160AWO	Cardiff Bus
D919HOU	Phil Anslow Travel	E283UCY	Brewers	EFX104T	Hawkes	F161AWO	Cardiff Bus
D920HOU	Phil Anslow Travel	E284UCY	Brewers	EHW288W	Wilkins Travel	F162AWO	Cardiff Bus
D967NCY	Hawkes	E285UCY	Brewers	EON827V	Glyn Williams	F163AWO	Cardiff Bus
D985ARE	Shamrock	E286UCY	Brewers	EPC916V	Ken Hopkins	F164AWO	Cardiff Bus
D986ARE	Shamrock	E287UCY	S W T	ERC882J	East End	F164JOD	Wilkins Travel
D987ARE	Shamrock	E288VEP	Brewers	ERC883J	East End	F165AWO	Cardiff Bus
D989ARE	Shamrock	E289VEP	S W T	ERW265T	Watts	F210AKG	Shamrock
DAD258T	Phil Anslow Travel	E290VEP	S W T	EWN992W	S W T	F223RJX	Ferris Holidays
DAE511K	Phil Anslow Travel	E291VEP	S W T	EWN994W	S W T	F224RJX	Ferris Holidays
DAK201V	Red & White	E292TAX	Red & White	EWN995W	S W T	F230DGB	Phil Anslow Travel
DAR119T	S W T	E292VEP	S W T	EWR654Y	Brewers	F231CNY	Cardiff Bus
DAR131T	S W T	E293VEP	S W T	EWR656Y	Rhondda	F232CNY	Cardiff Bus
DBV26W	Red & White	E295VEP	S W T	EWR657Y	Rhondda	F232OFP	Phil Anslow Travel
DDW433V	Red & White	E296VEP	S W T	EWW219T	Express	F233CNY	Cardiff Bus
DDW434V	Red & White	E297VEP	S W T	EWW945Y	Brewers	F233SMC	Castell Coaches
DDW530V	Shamrock	E298VEP	S W T	EYA251X	Express	F234CNY	Cardiff Bus
DEM821Y	Cardiff Bus	E299VEP	S W T	EYP30V	Hawkes	F235CNY	Cardiff Bus
DEM822Y	Cardiff Bus	E300VEP	S W T	F22CWO	Capitol Coaches	F236CNY	Cardiff Bus
DFB680W	Coastal Continental	E301VEP	S W T	F23CWO	Capitol Coaches	F237CNY	Cardiff Bus
DGS681X	Ferris Holidays	E302VEP	S W T	F25CWO	Capitol Coaches	F238CNY	Cardiff Bus
DHE696V	Ken Hopkins	E303VEP	S W T	F41YHB	Newport	F239CNY	Cardiff Bus
DKG321V	Watts	E304VEP	S W T	F42YHB	Newport	F240CNY	Cardiff Bus
DLJ113L	T R C	E305OMG	White Lion	F43YHB	Newport	F241CNY	Cardiff Bus
DMA515K	Hawthorn	E305VEP	S W T	F44YHB	Newport	F242CNY	Cardiff Bus
DMS20V	Red & White	E306VEP	S W T	F45YHB	Newport	F243CNY	Cardiff Bus
DMS22V	Red & White	E308HPU	Rhondda	F46YHB	Newport	F243OFP	Red & White
DNK428T	Wheadon's G'hound	E309HPU	Rhondda	F50ACL	Rhondda	F244CNY	Cardiff Bus
DNP444W	Phil Anslow Travel	E316HLO	Rhondda	F51ACL	Rhondda	F245CNY	Cardiff Bus
DNY534V	I B T	E320OMG	Glyn Williams	F58YBO	Phil Anslow Travel	F246CNY	Cardiff Bus
DSV520	Phillips	E321TTX	Edwards Coaches	F74DCW	Red & White	F247CNY	Cardiff Bus
DUP743S	Burrows	E380MPX	Watts	F79CJC	Howells Coaches	F248CNY	Cardiff Bus

The South Wales Bus Handbook

Reg	Operator	Reg	Operator	Reg	Operator	Reg	Operator
F248VBX	Wheadon's G'hound	F921MTM	Harris	G354JTH	S W T	GIL6241	Hawkes
F304JFT	Burrows	F961XWM	Shamrock	G355JTH	S W T	GMS282S	Henley's
F307AWN	S W T	F962XWM	Shamrock	G356JTH	S W T	GNY433C	Phillips
F308AWN	S W T	F963XWM	Shamrock	G357JTH	S W T	GOI5120	Llynfi Coaches
F309AWN	S W T	F964XWM	Shamrock	G358JTH	S W T	GRY626N	Martin
F310AWN	S W T	F982EDS	Harris	G359JTH	S W T	GSU9T	Hawthorn
F311AWN	S W T	F998XOV	Howells Coaches	G360JTH	S W T	GTG779W	Henley's
F312AWN	S W T	FAX69V	T R C	G361JTH	S W T	GTX738W	Red & White
F313AWN	S W T	FBO305L	Len Hopkins	G365JTH	S W T	GTX741W	Rhondda
F314AWN	S W T	FCY598W	T R C	G366JTH	S W T	GTX743W	Red & White
F315AWN	S W T	FDN583S	Thomas Coaches	G367MEP	S W T	GTX747W	Red & White
F316AWN	S W T	FEL11V	Edwards Coaches	G368MEP	S W T	GTX748W	Red & White
F317AWN	S W T	FEV449Y	Rees Travel	G369MEP	S W T	GTX750W	Red & White
F318AWN	Brewers	FHO86W	Thomas Coaches	G370CAJ	Shamrock	GTX753W	Red & White
F318AWN	S W T	FIL8541	Hawthorn	G370MEP	S W T	GTX756W	Edwards Coaches
F319AWN	S W T	FRJ243D	Edwards Coaches	G371MEP	S W T	GWU562T	Porthcawl Omnibus
F320AWN	S W T	FUA394Y	Watts	G372MEP	S W T	H49NDU	Cardiff Bus
F321AWN	S W T	FUJ900V	Edwards Coaches	G373MEP	S W T	H58GLP	Cyril Evans
F322AWN	S W T	FUS169L	Diamond Glantawe	G416WFP	Edwards Coaches	H59PNY	Newport
F323DCY	S W T	FUT181V	Diamond Glantawe	G450DSB	Capitol Coaches	H61PNY	Newport
F324DCY	S W T	FUT186V	Diamond Glantawe	G517LWU	Capitol Coaches	H62PNY	Newport
F325DCY	S W T	FWF358V	Ken Hopkins	G545RVJ	Castell Coaches	H63PNY	Newport
F326DCY	S W T	FXI8505	Llynfi Coaches	G584RNC	Venture Travel	H64PNY	Newport
F327DCY	S W T	G21CSG	Red & White	G601KTX	Cardiff Bus	H122YGG	Morris Travel
F328FCY	S W T	G24CSG	Red & White	G602KTX	Cardiff Bus	H159EJU	Red & White
F329FCY	S W T	G33HDW	Shamrock	G603KTX	Cardiff Bus	H160PNY	Newport
F330FCY	S W T	G34OHS	Harris	G604KTX	Cardiff Bus	H168OTG	Cardiff Bus
F331FCY	S W T	G47FKG	Newport	G605KTX	Cardiff Bus	H169OTG	Cardiff Bus
F332FCY	S W T	G48FKG	Newport	G606KTX	Cardiff Bus	H170OTG	Cardiff Bus
F333FCY	S W T	G49FKG	Newport	G607KTX	Cardiff Bus	H171OTG	Cardiff Bus
F334FCY	S W T	G50FKG	Newport	G654EVN	Shamrock	H172RBO	Cardiff Bus
F335FCY	S W T	G51FKG	Newport	G689KNW	Rhondda	H173RBO	Cardiff Bus
F336FCY	S W T	G52FKG	Newport	G738LEP	Diamond Glantawe	H174RBO	Cardiff Bus
F337FCY	S W T	G53KTX	Newport	G780HFV	Brian Issac	H175RBO	Cardiff Bus
F338FCY	S W T	G54KTX	Newport	G797RNC	Phil Anslow Travel	H185EJF	Watts
F338XOV	John's Travel	G54RTO	Watts	G798RNC	Phil Anslow Travel	H220GKK	Thomas Coaches
F339FCY	S W T	G55KTX	Newport	G805XLO	Rhondda	H258GRY	Cyril Evans
F340FCY	S W T	G55RTO	Watts	G830UMU	Glyn Williams	H301PAX	Red & White
F341FCY	S W T	G56KTX	Newport	G837GNV	Jones of Bryncethin	H335LAN	Porthcawl Omnibus
F342FCY	S W T	G57KTX	Newport	G841CLV	Shamrock	H366NCY	Llynfi Coaches
F343FCY	S W T	G58KTX	Newport	G841PNW	Brewers	H368NDW	Shamrock
F349TSX	I B T	G116CSJ	Thomas Coaches	G844GNV	Hawthorn	H374OTH	S W T
F427EMB	Shamrock	G117CSJ	Thomas Coaches	G847VAY	Shamrock	H375OTH	S W T
F428EMB	Shamrock	G117XRE	Capitol Coaches	G923LTH	Pullman Coaches	H376OTH	S W T
F511CKU	Llynfi Coaches	G120AAD	Ferris Holidays	G991OKJ	Wilkins Travel	H377OTH	S W T
F544JRO	John's Travel	G166HWO	Cardiff Bus	GAX137W	I B T	H378OTH	S W T
F546EJA	Brewers	G167HWO	Cardiff Bus	GAX138W	Pullman Coaches	H379OTH	S W T
F575KVL	Edwards Coaches	G168XJF	Harris	GBD888T	Llynfi Coaches	H380OTH	S W T
F594BTG	Castell Coaches	G249HUH	Cardiff Bus	GBO241W	Llynfi Coaches	H381OTH	S W T
F598BTG	Watts	G250HUH	Cardiff Bus	GCJ420N	Martin	H382TTH	S W T
F601AWN	Brewers	G251HUH	Cardiff Bus	GDB174N	Edwards Coaches	H390GAV	Llynfi Coaches
F602AWN	Brewers	G252HUH	Cardiff Bus	GDE383W	Pullman Coaches	H492OHB	Shamrock
F603AWN	Brewers	G253HUH	Cardiff Bus	GFO770X	Hawthorn	H493OHB	Shamrock
F604AWN	Brewers	G254HUH	Cardiff Bus	GGM71W	Rhondda	H494OHB	Shamrock
F605AWN	Brewers	G255HUH	Cardiff Bus	GGM73W	Rhondda	H556TUG	Shamrock
F606AWN	Brewers	G256HUH	Cardiff Bus	GHB146N	Red & White	H607UWR	Castell Coaches
F607AWN	S W T	G257HUH	Cardiff Bus	GHB148N	Red & White	H610UWR	Capitol Coaches
F608AWN	Brewers	G258HUH	Cardiff Bus	GHC521N	Edwards Coaches	H611UWR	Capitol Coaches
F613PWS	Brian Issac	G259HUH	Cardiff Bus	GHJ384L	Diamond Glantawe	H687UHH	Shamrock
F623CWJ	Ferris Holidays	G300JEP	Burrows	GHM802N	Diamond Glantawe	H688UHH	Shamrock
F631CWJ	Ferris Holidays	G344GEP	S W T	GHM829N	Diamond Glantawe	H689UHH	Shamrock
F664TBE	Shamrock	G345GEP	S W T	GHM880N	Diamond Glantawe	H690UHH	Shamrock
F670DBO	Shamrock	G346GEP	S W T	GHV48N	Diamond Glantawe	H787NUH	Shamrock
F671DBO	Shamrock	G347GEP	S W T	GHV52N	Diamond Glantawe	H788NUH	Shamrock
F672DBO	Shamrock	G348JTH	S W T	GHV59N	Diamond Glantawe	H789NUH	Shamrock
F757GUS	Harris	G349JTH	S W T	GHV114N	Diamond Glantawe	H818RWJ	Thomas Coaches
F815CWJ	Rhondda	G350JTH	S W T	GHV995N	Venture Travel	H825ERV	Brewers
F852LHS	I B T	G351JTH	S W T	GIJ330	Jones of Bryncethin	H852OWN	S W T
F871CNY	Ferris Holidays	G352JTH	S W T	GIL2409	White Lion	H853OWN	S W T
F898LCJ	Martin	G353JTH	S W T	GIL6240	Hawkes	H859NOC	Brian Issac

IBT's influx of Mercedes-Benz minibuses during 1995 comprised three new and five second-hand purchases, four of which came from Kelvin Central. These included the coach version seen on page 54 and three Alexander Sprints such as 06, F349TSX. *John Jones*

H904AHS	Castell Coaches	IIL1829	S W T	J268UDW	Cardiff Bus	J608VDW	Cardiff Bus
H907XGA	I B T	IIL2565	Wheadon's G'hound	J269UDW	Cardiff Bus	J609VDW	Cardiff Bus
H920WMW	Llynfi Coaches	IIL2566	Wheadon's G'hound	J270UDW	Cardiff Bus	J610VDW	Cardiff Bus
H974PCY	Llynfi Coaches	IIL3481	I B T	J271UDW	Cardiff Bus	J783KHD	Cyril Evans
HBD165N	East End	IIL6234	Diamond Glantawe	J272UWO	Cardiff Bus	J797MHF	Rhondda
HBD166N	East End	IIL6235	Diamond Glantawe	J273UWO	Cardiff Bus	J832KHD	Cyril Evans
HDL410N	East End	IIL6443	I B T	J274UWO	Cardiff Bus	J901MAF	Brewers
HGD869L	Diamond Glantawe	IIL6541	Ken Hopkins	J275UWO	Cardiff Bus	J905UBO	Newport
HHH371V	Glyn Williams	IIL7331	I B T	J276UWO	Cardiff Bus	J916WVC	Brewers
HHJ374Y	Brewers	IIL8586	Merlyn's	J277UWO	Cardiff Bus	JBO461N	Len Hopkins
HHJ377Y	Brewers	J2SWT	S W T	J278UWO	Cardiff Bus	JBZ6925	Henley's
HHJ379Y	Brewers	J3SWT	S W T	J279UWO	Cardiff Bus	JBZ6926	Mansell David
HHW915L	Phil Anslow Travel	J4SWT	S W T	J281UWO	Cardiff Bus	JDB952V	Howells Coaches
HHW917L	Phil Anslow Travel	J5SWT	S W T	J282UWO	Cardiff Bus	JEC592T	Ken Hopkins
HIL3188	Rhondda	J23VWO	Castell Coaches	J283UWO	Cardiff Bus	JHE139W	Cardiff Bluebird
HIL7540	Morris Travel	J40MCL	Merlyn's	J284UWO	Cardiff Bus	JHE141W	Cardiff Bluebird
HIL7542	Morris Travel	J42VWO	Ferris Holidays	J285UWO	Cardiff Bus	JHE143W	Cardiff Bluebird
HIL8285	Phil Anslow Travel	J43VWO	Ferris Holidays	J286UWO	Cardiff Bus	JHE163W	Cardiff Bluebird
HIL8410	Red & White	J96NJT	Newport	J292TTX	Edwards Coaches	JHE164W	Cardiff Bluebird
HIL8914	Diamond Glantawe	J145UCY	Llynfi Coaches	J302TUH	Red & White	JIB506	Cyril Evans
HIW679	Cyril Evans	J174GGG	Shamrock	J303TUH	Red & White	JIL2432	White Lion
HJI980	Brian Issac	J176WAX	Cardiff Bus	J304UKG	Red & White	JIL2433	White Lion
HJP479V	Hawkes	J177WAX	Cardiff Bus	J305UKG	Red & White	JIL2665	Hawthorn
HNB40N	Edwards Coaches	J178WAX	Cardiff Bus	J306UKG	Red & White	JIL3253	Venture Travel
HNU125N	Diamond Glantawe	J179WAX	Cardiff Bus	J307UKG	Red & White	JIL3254	Venture Travel
HRN923N	Express	J180WAX	Cardiff Bus	J331TTX	Thomas Coaches	JIL3585	Diamond Glantawe
HTG354N	Red & White	J181WAX	Cardiff Bus	J344MBX	Castell Coaches	JIL3586	Diamond Glantawe
HTG557K	Wilkins Travel	J182WAX	Cardiff Bus	J375WWK	Brewers	JIL7652	Ken Hopkins
HUX83V	Rees Travel	J212XKY	Thomas Coaches	J378MBX	Merlyn's	JIL7903	Phillips
HUX84V	Rees Travel	J261UDW	Cardiff Bus	J379MBX	Merlyn's	JJG5P	Burrows
HVC8V	Wheadon's G'hound	J262UDW	Cardiff Bus	J404NBA	Perry's Supreme	JKE102L	Waterhall
HVD588N	Ken Hopkins	J263UDW	Cardiff Bus	J454JRH	Rhondda	JKE103L	Waterhall
IIB9140	Phil Anslow Travel	J264UDW	Cardiff Bus	J469NJU	Merlyn's	JKV104N	Hawkes
IIB9890	Pullman Coaches	J265UDW	Cardiff Bus	J580VTH	S W T	JMB401T	T R C
IIJ5426	Diamond Glantawe	J266UDW	Cardiff Bus	J581VTH	S W T	JMR858W	Wheadon's G'hound
IIL1828	S W T	J267UDW	Cardiff Bus	J582VTH	S W T	JNB150N	Rhondda

118

Among Rhondda's varied fleet of Dennis Darts one unique vehicle stands out, 97, K97XNY. Originally delivered with a Wright Handy-bus body it was burnt out in October 1994 at Talbot Green bus station. It was despatched to Plaxtons for rebodying and emerged with a Pointer body later the following year. It is currently allocated to Caerphilly Busways.

JNJ365V	Hawkes	K109YTX	Newport	K404BAX	Brewers	KPP615V	Wheadon's G'hound
JRT710N	Wheadon's G'hound	K183YDW	Cardiff Bus	K405BAX	Brewers	KSO64P	Shamrock
JSC884E	Diamond Glantawe	K184YDW	Cardiff Bus	K406BAX	Brewers	KUC144P	Diamond Glantawe
JSJ426W	Hawkes	K185YDW	Cardiff Bus	K407BAX	Brewers	KUC222P	Diamond Glantawe
JTH769P	Hawkes	K186YDW	Cardiff Bus	K408BAX	Brewers	KUC237P	Diamond Glantawe
JUH228W	Merlyn's	K187YDW	Cardiff Bus	K409BAX	Brewers	KUX230W	Rhondda
JVS929N	Jones of Bryncethin	K205OHS	Phil Anslow Travel	K410BAX	Brewers	KVC384V	Arthur Thomas
JWE244W	Brewers	K206OHS	Phil Anslow Travel	K451VAY	Shamrock	KVD442P	Merlyn's
JWE245W	Brian Issac	K309YKG	Red & White	K486BCY	Diamond Glantawe	KVD456P	Hawkes
JWE247W	Brian Issac	K310YKG	Red & White	K487BCY	Diamond Glantawe	KWG433W	Brian Issac
JWE248W	Brian Issac	K311YKG	Red & White	K537CWN	Diamond Glantawe	KWN815P	Diamond Glantawe
JWE249W	Brewers	K312YKG	Red & White	K538CWN	Diamond Glantawe	KXI169	White Lion
JWE250W	Brian Issac	K313YKG	Red & White	K539CWN	Diamond Glantawe	KXI318	White Lion
JWE251W	Brewers	K314YKG	Red & White	K540CWN	Diamond Glantawe	KXI366	White Lion
JXI1753	Ken Hopkins	K315YKG	Red & White	K586MHY	Shamrock	KYL828X	Jones of Bryncethin
K9BMS	Brewers	K316YKG	Red & White	K588MHY	Shamrock	L2PCL	Pullman Coaches
K10BMS	Brewers	K317YKG	Red & White	K589TRY	Shamrock	L4USE	I B T
K11BMS	Brewers	K318YKG	Red & White	K590TRY	Shamrock	L6BMS	Brewers
K12BMS	Brewers	K319YKG	Red & White	K927AEP	Shamrock	L8BMS	Brewers
K13BMS	Brewers	K320FYG	Rhondda	K928AEP	Shamrock	L14BMS	Brewers
K82BWN	S W T	K320YKG	Red & White	K929AEP	Shamrock	L38DBC	Shamrock
K91BNY	Rhondda	K321YKG	Red & White	K930AEP	Shamrock	L58YJF	Wheadon's G'hound
K92BNY	Rhondda	K322YKG	Red & White	KAD353V	Arthur Thomas	L68EKG	Newport
K93BNY	Rhondda	K323YKG	Red & White	KBO601P	Len Hopkins	L69EKG	Newport
K94AAX	Rhondda	K324YKG	Red & White	KDW327P	Glyn Williams	L71EKG	Newport
K95AAX	Rhondda	K325YKG	Red & White	KEC976X	Wilkins Travel	L73EKG	Newport
K96AAX	Rhondda	K330YDW	Thomas Coaches	KEH878N	Waterhall	L79CWO	Rhondda
K97RGA	Glyn Williams	K331YDW	Thomas Coaches	KIB1767	I B T	L81CWO	Rhondda
K97XNY	Rhondda	K332YDW	Thomas Coaches	KIW3766	Wilkins Travel	L82CWO	Rhondda
K98XNY	Rhondda	K365TJF	Shamrock	KJD11P	Diamond Glantawe	L83CWO	Rhondda
K104YTX	Newport	K366TJF	Shamrock	KJD412P	Henley's	L84CWO	Rhondda
K105YTX	Newport	K401BAX	Brewers	KJD542P	Shamrock	L85CWO	Rhondda
K106YTX	Newport	K402BAX	Brewers	KMH39	Ken Hopkins	L86CWO	Rhondda
K107YTX	Newport	K402EDT	Rhondda	KMW179P	Brian Issac	L87CWO	Rhondda
K108YTX	Newport	K403BAX	Brewers	KOW66Y	Hawthorn	L89CWO	Rhondda

Reg	Operator	Reg	Operator	Reg	Operator	Reg	Operator
L101GBO	Cardiff Bus	L509HCY	S W T	L818HCY	S W T	M37KAX	Bebb
L102GBO	Cardiff Bus	L510HCY	S W T	L819HCY	S W T	M38KAX	Bebb
L103GBO	Cardiff Bus	L511HCY	S W T	L820HCY	S W T	M39KAX	Bebb
L104GBO	Cardiff Bus	L512HCY	S W T	L821HCY	S W T	M41KAX	Bebb
L105GBO	Cardiff Bus	L513HCY	S W T	L822HCY	S W T	M42KAX	Bebb
L106GBO	Cardiff Bus	L514HCY	S W T	L823HCY	S W T	M43KAX	Bebb
L141AHS	Castell Coaches	L515HCY	S W T	L824HCY	S W T	M45KAX	Bebb
L170EKG	Newport	L516HCY	S W T	L825HCY	S W T	M64HHB	Rhondda
L172EKG	Newport	L517HCY	S W T	L839FTX	Llynfi Coaches	M65HHB	Rhondda
L188DDW	Cardiff Bus	L518HCY	S W T	L839MWT	Rhondda	M65KTG	Newport
L189DDW	Cardiff Bus	L519HCY	S W T	L840MWT	Rhondda	M67HHB	Rhondda
L190DDW	Cardiff Bus	L520HCY	S W T	L844JCY	S W T	M67KTG	Newport
L191DDW	Cardiff Bus	L521HCY	S W T	L913UGA	Phil Anslow Travel	M68HHB	Rhondda
L192DDW	Cardiff Bus	L522HCY	S W T	L914UGA	Phil Anslow Travel	M69HHB	Rhondda
L193DDW	Cardiff Bus	L523HCY	S W T	L920UGA	Glyn Williams	M71HHB	Rhondda
L194DDW	Cardiff Bus	L524HCY	S W T	L927UGA	Phil Anslow Travel	M72HHB	Rhondda
L195DDW	Cardiff Bus	L525JEP	S W T	L928UGA	Phil Anslow Travel	M73HHB	Rhondda
L196DDW	Cardiff Bus	L526JEP	S W T	L929UGA	Phil Anslow Travel	M74HHB	Rhondda
L197DDW	Cardiff Bus	L527JEP	S W T	L936KSG	Phil Anslow Travel	M74KTG	Newport
L217ETG	Cyril Evans	L528JEP	S W T	L937KSG	Phil Anslow Travel	M75HHB	Rhondda
L218ETG	Ferris Holidays	L529JEP	S W T	L957JGS	Shamrock	M75KTG	Newport
L270EHB	Rhondda	L530JEP	S W T	L965DBO	Silverline	M76HHB	Rhondda
L287ETG	Cardiff Bus	L531JEP	S W T	LAK306W	Ken Hopkins	M76KTG	Newport
L288ETG	Cardiff Bus	L532JEP	S W T	LAX72P	Diamond Glantawe	M78HHB	Rhondda
L289ETG	Cardiff Bus	L533JEP	S W T	LBO501X	Cardiff Bus	M91JHB	Phil Anslow Travel
L290ETG	Cardiff Bus	L534JEP	S W T	LBO728P	I B T	M92JHB	Phil Anslow Travel
L291ETG	Cardiff Bus	L535JEP	S W T	LBO729P	I B T	M93JHB	Phil Anslow Travel
L292ETG	Cardiff Bus	L536JEP	S W T	LBO730P	I B T	M100CBB	Cardiff Bluebird
L293ETG	Cardiff Bus	L536XNR	Shamrock	LHT170L	Phil Anslow Travel	M107JHB	Cardiff Bus
L326CHB	Red & White	L537JEP	S W T	LHT173L	Phil Anslow Travel	M107NEP	S W T
L327CHB	Red & White	L537XNR	Shamrock	LHT729P	Coastal Continental	M108JHB	Cardiff Bus
L328CHB	Red & White	L538JEP	S W T	LIL3934	I B T	M108NEP	S W T
L329CHB	Red & White	L539JEP	S W T	LIL5068	Brewers	M109JHB	Cardiff Bus
L331CHB	Red & White	L540JEP	S W T	LIL5069	Brewers	M109PWN	S W T
L334DTG	Thomas Coaches	L541JEP	S W T	LIL5070	Brewers	M110KBO	Cardiff Bus
L334FWO	Red & White	L542JEP	S W T	LIL5071	Brewers	M110PWN	S W T
L335DTG	Thomas Coaches	L543JEP	S W T	LIL7332	Morris Travel	M111PWN	S W T
L335FWO	Red & White	L544JEP	S W T	LIL7493	Diamond Glantawe	M112KBO	Cardiff Bus
L336DTG	Thomas Coaches	L544XUT	Ferris Holidays	LIL9407	Edwards Coaches	M113KBO	Cardiff Bus
L336FWO	Red & White	L545JEP	S W T	LIL9969	Shamrock	M114KBO	Cardiff Bus
L337DTG	Thomas Coaches	L546JEP	S W T	LIL9970	Shamrock	M115KBO	Cardiff Bus
L337FWO	Red & White	L547JEP	S W T	LIL9971	Shamrock	M116KBO	Cardiff Bus
L338DTG	Thomas Coaches	L548JEP	S W T	LIL9972	Shamrock	M117KBO	Cardiff Bus
L338FWO	Red & White	L549JEP	S W T	LIL9973	Shamrock	M118KBO	Cardiff Bus
L339FWO	Red & White	L550JEP	S W T	LIL9974	Shamrock	M119KBO	Cardiff Bus
L340FWO	Red & White	L552XNR	Shamrock	LIL9975	Shamrock	M120KBO	Cardiff Bus
L341FWO	Red & White	L553XNR	Shamrock	LIL9976	Shamrock	M121KBO	Cardiff Bus
L342FWO	Red & White	L559YYS	Castell Coaches	LMB909P	Edwards Coaches	M122KBO	Cardiff Bus
L343FWO	Red & White	L601FKG	Brewers	LNV795	Porthcawl Omnibus	M123KBO	Cardiff Bus
L351YNR	Ferris Holidays	L602FKG	Brewers	LPP347V	Edwards Coaches	M124KBO	Cardiff Bus
L354MKU	Castell Coaches	L603FKG	Brewers	LRB200W	Glyn Williams	M125KBO	Cardiff Bus
L355YNR	Phil Anslow Travel	L604FKG	Brewers	LRB212W	Glyn Williams	M126KBO	Cardiff Bus
L361ANR	Shamrock	L605FKG	Brewers	LRB216W	Glyn Williams	M127KBO	Cardiff Bus
L362ANR	Shamrock	L606FKG	Brewers	LTA879W	Perry's Supreme	M128KBO	Cardiff Bus
L364GTH	S W T	L607FKG	Brewers	LUA263V	Express	M129KBO	Cardiff Bus
L414SFL	Silverline	L608FKG	Brewers	LVS419V	Nelson's Travel	M130KBO	Cardiff Bus
L465XNR	Shamrock	L681GKG	Thomas Coaches	LWG533W	Porthcawl Omnibus	M131KBO	Cardiff Bus
L466XNR	Shamrock	L685CDD	Red & White	LWN790X	Porthcawl Omnibus	M132KBO	Cardiff Bus
L467XNR	Shamrock	L697CNR	Wheadon's G'hound	M23JDW	Bebb	M133KBO	Cardiff Bus
L468XNR	Shamrock	L701FWO	Red & White	M24JDW	Bebb	M166KTG	Newport
L500BWN	Brian Issac	L702FWO	Red & White	M26HNY	Bebb	M200CBB	Cardiff Bluebird
L501HCY	S W T	L703FWO	Red & White	M27HNY	Bebb	M201RHB	Henley's
L502HCY	S W T	L704FWO	Red & White	M28HNY	Bebb	M242JHB	Glyn Williams
L503HCY	S W T	L705FWO	Red & White	M29HNY	Bebb	M243JHB	Glyn Williams
L504HCY	S W T	L706FWO	Red & White	M31KAX	Bebb	M244JHB	Glyn Williams
L505HCY	S W T	L707FWO	Red & White	M31KUT	Shamrock	M252KNR	Shamrock
L506GEP	S W T	L708FWO	Red & White	M32KAX	Bebb	M303KRY	Ferris Holidays
L506HCY	S W T	L775GNM	Shamrock	M34KAX	Bebb	M330JHB	Thomas Coaches
L507HCY	S W T	L816HCY	S W T	M35KAX	Bebb	M344JBO	Red & White
L508HCY	S W T	L817HCY	S W T	M36KAX	Bebb	M345JBO	Red & White

120

M346JBO	Red & White	M943JBO	Red & White	N47MDW	Bebb	N376PNY	Red & White
M346MCY	Diamond Glantawe	M944JBO	Red & White	N48MDW	Bebb	N377PNY	Red & White
M347JBO	Red & White	M945JBO	Red & White	N49MDW	Bebb	N378PNY	Red & White
M347MCY	Diamond Glantawe	M946JBO	Red & White	N51MDW	Bebb	N379PNY	Red & White
M348JBO	Red & White	M947JBO	Red & White	N52MDW	Bebb	N380PNY	Red & White
M348MCY	Diamond Glantawe	M948JBO	Red & White	N53MDW	Bebb	N381PNY	Red & White
M349JBO	Red & White	M949JBO	Red & White	N54MDW	Bebb	N382PNY	Red & White
M350JBO	Red & White	M950JBO	Red & White	N56MDW	Bebb	N383PNY	Red & White
M351JBO	Red & White	M951JBO	Red & White	N57MDW	Bebb	N384PNY	Red & White
M352JBO	Red & White	M982KKG	Shamrock	N58MDW	Bebb	N417UWN	Phil Anslow Travel
M353JBO	Red & White	M983KKG	Shamrock	N59MDW	Bebb	N418UWN	Phil Anslow Travel
M354JBO	Red & White	M984KKG	Shamrock	N61MDW	Bebb	N419UWN	Phil Anslow Travel
M355JBO	Red & White	M985KKG	Shamrock	N62MDW	Bebb	N461OTX	Shamrock
M356JBO	Red & White	M986KKG	Shamrock	N62MTG	Rhondda	N462OTX	Shamrock
M357JBO	Red & White	M987KKG	Shamrock	N63MDW	Bebb	N463OTX	Shamrock
M358JBO	Red & White	M997CYS	S W T	N63MTG	Rhondda	N511PNY	Shamrock
M359JBO	Red & White	MAP340W	Cyril Evans	N64MDW	Bebb	N512PNY	Shamrock
M360JBO	Red & White	MAP341W	Cyril Evans	N65MDW	Bebb	N513PNY	Shamrock
M361LAX	Red & White	MAP342W	Cyril Evans	N67MDW	Bebb	N550MTG	Rhondda
M362LAX	Red & White	MAU141P	Waterhall	N68MDW	Bebb	N551MTG	Rhondda
M363LAX	Red & White	MAU618P	Cardiff Bluebird	N69MDW	Bebb	N551UCY	S W T
M364LAX	Red & White	MAU619P	Cardiff Bluebird	N71MDW	Bebb	N552UCY	S W T
M365LAX	Red & White	MAU620P	Cardiff Bluebird	N78PDW	Newport	N553UCY	S W T
M366LAX	Red & White	MAU621P	Cardiff Bluebird	N79PDW	Newport	N554UCY	S W T
M367LAX	Red & White	MCO253H	G M	N81PDW	Newport	N555UCY	S W T
M368LAX	Red & White	MCY85G	Wilkins Travel	N82PDW	Newport	N556UCY	S W T
M369LAX	Red & White	MCY111X	Edwards Coaches	N83PDW	Newport	N557UCY	S W T
M370LAX	Red & White	MCY839X	Diamond Glantawe	N91SKG	Bebb	N558UCY	S W T
M371LAX	Red & White	MDV143W	Brian Issac	N92SKG	Bebb	N559UCY	S W T
M425JNY	Shamrock	MFN114R	Red & White	N93SKG	Bebb	N561UCY	S W T
M426JNY	Shamrock	MHJ721V	Glyn Williams	N94SKG	Bebb	N562UCY	S W T
M485HBC	Wheadon's G'hound	MHJ729V	Glyn Williams	N95SKG	Bebb	N563UCY	S W T
M528KTG	Glyn Williams	MHJ732V	Glyn Williams	N103BHL	Castell Coaches	N564UCY	S W T
M542JHB	Edwards Coaches	MHS30P	Cardiff Bluebird	N112EWJ	S W T	N565UCY	S W T
M562JTG	Rhondda	MIL2407	Edwards Coaches	N112OBO	Phil Anslow Travel	N566UCY	S W T
M625KKG	Rhondda	MIL3292	Len Hopkins	N113VWN	S W T	N567UCY	S W T
M710HBC	Shamrock	MIL3293	Len Hopkins	N114VWN	S W T	N568UCY	S W T
M711HBC	Shamrock	MKH59A	Brewers	N115VWN	S W T	N571OUH	I B T
M717NCY	Diamond Glantawe	MKH69A	Brewers	N134PTG	Cardiff Bus	N572OUH	I B T
M720LTG	Edwards Coaches	MKH87A	Brewers	N135PTG	Cardiff Bus	N573OUH	I B T
M737JKG	Shamrock	MKH98A	Brewers	N136PTG	Cardiff Bus	N595DWY	Ferris Holidays
M738JKG	Shamrock	MKH487A	S W T	N137PTG	Cardiff Bus	N609MHB	Brewers
M750LAX	Red & White	MKH678A	Edwards Coaches	N138PTG	Cardiff Bus	N610MHB	Brewers
M751LAX	Red & White	MKH690A	Edwards Coaches	N139PTG	Cardiff Bus	N611MHB	Brewers
M752LAX	Red & White	MKH730A	Edwards Coaches	N140PTG	Cardiff Bus	N612MHB	Brewers
M753LAX	Red & White	MKH748A	Ferris Holidays	N141PTG	Cardiff Bus	N613MHB	Brewers
M754LAX	Red & White	MKH824A	Edwards Coaches	N142PTG	Cardiff Bus	N614MHB	Brewers
M755LAX	Red & White	MMB145T	Express	N143PTG	Cardiff Bus	N615MHB	Brewers
M756LAX	Red & White	MMJ549V	Wheadon's G'hound	N143XEG	Shamrock	N616MHB	Brewers
M757LAX	Red & White	MRJ102W	Edwards Coaches	N144XEG	Shamrock	N617MHB	Brewers
M758LAX	Red & White	MSO13W	Red & White	N145XEG	Shamrock	N618MHB	Brewers
M759LAX	Red & White	MSO14W	Red & White	N151MTG	Rhondda	N707MWO	Capitol Coaches
M760LAX	Red & White	MUE313V	Hawkes	N152MTG	Rhondda	N714CYC	Diamond Glantawe
M761LAX	Red & White	MUS281F	Edwards Coaches	N153MTG	Rhondda	N715CYC	Diamond Glantawe
M762LAX	Red & White	MUT253V	Diamond Glantawe	N154MTG	Rhondda	N716CYC	Diamond Glantawe
M763LAX	Red & White	MUT254V	Diamond Glantawe	N155MTG	Rhondda	N717CYC	Diamond Glantawe
M764LAX	Red & White	MUT255V	Diamond Glantawe	N156MTG	Rhondda	N731PWO	Capitol Coaches
M765RAX	Red & White	MUT261V	Diamond Glantawe	N157MTG	Rhondda	N753VCY	Pullman Coaches
M766RAX	Red & White	MUT262V	Diamond Glantawe	N158MTG	Rhondda	N755NAY	Shamrock
M767RAX	Red & White	MUT263V	Diamond Glantawe	N159MTG	Rhondda	N808MWO	Capitol Coaches
M768RAX	Red & White	MYD215V	Wilkins Travel	N160MTG	Rhondda	N825NUH	Cyril Evans
M769RAX	Red & White	N2PCL	Pullman Coaches	N180PDW	Newport	N827XRD	Ferris Holidays
M770RAX	Red & White	N23OBO	Cardiff Bus	N251NNR	Wheadon's G'hound	N854PDW	Shamrock
M848LTX	Capitol Coaches	N24OBO	Cardiff Bus	N253NNR	Wheadon's G'hound	N855PDW	Shamrock
M851JHB	Shamrock	N25OBO	Cardiff Bus	N254NNR	Wheadon's G'hound	N856PDW	Shamrock
M852JHB	Shamrock	N26OBO	Cardiff Bus	N313VWN	Brian Issac	N857PDW	Shamrock
M866LNY	Rhondda	N27OBO	Cardiff Bus	N372PNY	Red & White	N859PDY	Silverline
M940JBO	Red & White	N28OBO	Cardiff Bus	N373PNY	Red & White	NAT201V	Glyn Williams
M941JBO	Red & White	N29OBO	Cardiff Bus	N374PNY	Red & White	NAY429W	Perry's Supreme
M942JBO	Red & White	N46MDW	Bebb	N375PNY	Red & White	NBX190N	Hawthorn

Currently the oldest vehicle in the Nelsons Travel fleet is this 10-metre Leyland Leopard, RJI2724. The re-registration disguises its heritage as a Midland Red coach that subsequently operated with National Travel West , Western National and an independent in Weymouth. The Plaxton Elite style was used extensively for the front-line coaches of BET companies just prior to the formation of National Bus. *John Jones*

NBZ1844	Capitol Coaches	NIW5983	White Lion	NWO457R	Red & White	OJD239R	Howells Coaches
NCX25W	Hawthorn	NIW8291	Rhondda	NWO461R	Red & White	OJD354R	Thomas Coaches
NDW141X	Venture Travel	NJI3995	Ferris Holidays	NWO462R	Hawkes	OJD375R	Venture Travel
NDW401X	Cardiff Bus	NLJ97N	Hawthorn	NWO468R	Red & White	OJD462R	Venture Travel
NDW402X	Cardiff Bus	NLS987W	Red & White	OAE954M	Phil Anslow Travel	OJI5267	Wheadon's G'hound
NDW403X	Cardiff Bus	NNN399P	Hawthorn	OAX500M	Henley's	OJI9472	Jones of Bryncethin
NDW404X	Cardiff Bus	NNX285P	Hawkes	OAX615R	Wheadon's G'hound	OJI9474	Jones of Bryncethin
NDW405X	Cardiff Bus	NNY817L	Perry's Supreme	OAX974M	I B T	OJI9475	Jones of Bryncethin
NDW406X	Cardiff Bus	NOC403R	Thomas Coaches	OCU420R	Coastal Continental	OJI9477	Jones of Bryncethin
NDW407X	Cardiff Bus	NOC410R	Thomas Coaches	ODJ583W	Waterhall	OKG292R	Coastal Continental
NDW408X	Cardiff Bus	NOC412R	Thomas Coaches	ODJ598W	Morris Travel	OMA503V	Cyril Evans
NDW409X	Cardiff Bus	NOC493R	Thomas Coaches	ODJ605W	Morris Travel	ONN574P	Cardiff Bluebird
NDW410X	Cardiff Bus	NOE552R	Red & White	ODV405W	Welsh Dragon	ONV651Y	Morris Travel
NDW411X	Cardiff Bus	NOE572R	Red & White	OEH604M	Thomas Coaches	OPR511W	Castell Coaches
NDW412X	Cardiff Bus	NOE573R	Red & White	OEP792R	S W T	ORU236G	Edwards Coaches
NDW413X	Cardiff Bus	NOE576R	Red & White	OEP794R	Brewers	OSR206R	Red & White
NDW414X	Cardiff Bus	NPP345V	Phillips	OEP795R	Brewers	OSR207R	Red & White
NDW415X	Cardiff Bus	NRG164M	Phillips	OHV190Y	Wilkins Travel	OSR208R	Red & White
NDW416X	Cardiff Bus	NRG169M	Phillips	OHV193Y	Wilkins Travel	OSR209R	Red & White
NDW417X	Cardiff Bus	NRO266V	Edwards Coaches	OHV209Y	Wilkins Travel	OTO560M	Burrows
NDW418X	Cardiff Bus	NSJ4R	Hawkes	OIB5880	G M	OVV847R	East End
NEU430	White Lion	NSU638V	Len Hopkins	OIB6694	Hawthorn	OWN250R	Wilkins Travel
NFE313V	Arthur Thoma	NSX960T	Arthur Thomas	OIB7631	G M	OWU992W	Hawthorn
NGB103M	Diamond Glantawe	NTD118K	Diamond Glantawe	OIB7915	G M	PAA826	Len Hopkins
NHA259M	Shamrock	NTH162X	Edwards Coaches	OIB8587	Hawkes	PAG760H	Edwards Coaches
NIB3214	I B T	NTX577R	I B T	OIJ864	Wilkins Travel	PBC461W	Phillips
NIW2309	Rhondda	NWG990X	Martin	OJD196R	Howells Coaches	PDW484	Newport
NIW4810	Rhondda	NWO454R	Red & White	OJD234R	Howells Coaches	PDW99H	Edwards Coaches

East End of Clydach is one of the few last resting places of the Seddon RU saloons. A total of sixteen of these unusual machines were purchased between 1980 and 1991 although ten have since been dismantled or retained for spares for the six still in use. One of the Darlington dual-doored examples, WHN468M, is seen here at the depot in Clydach. *John Jones*

Reg	Operator	Reg	Operator	Reg	Operator	Reg	Operator
PHB309R	I B T	PTG99Y	Newport	RJI8718	Rees Travel	RSG825V	Red & White
PHB310R	I B T	PTG100Y	Newport	RJI8719	Rees Travel	RUH10Y	Newport
PHB901R	Perry's Supreme	PUJ998M	Nelson's Travel	RKG419Y	Cardiff Bus	RUH11Y	Newport
PHW985S	Red & White	PVV318	Welsh Dragon	RKG420Y	Cardiff Bus	RUH12Y	Newport
PJI3546	Nelson's Travel	PWL939W	Edwards Coaches	RKG421Y	Cardiff Bus	RUH13Y	Newport
PJI3547	Nelson's Travel	PXI8687	Ken Hopkins	RKG422Y	Cardiff Bus	RUH14Y	Newport
PJI3548	Nelson's Travel	RBO502Y	Cardiff Bus	RKG423Y	Cardiff Bus	RUH15Y	Newport
PJI3549	Nelson's Travel	RBO503Y	Cardiff Bus	RKG424Y	Cardiff Bus	RUH16Y	Newport
PJI3550	Nelson's Travel	RBO504Y	Cardiff Bus	RKG425Y	Cardiff Bus	RUH17Y	Newport
PKG702Y	Henley's	RBO505Y	Cardiff Bus	RKG426Y	Cardiff Bus	RUH18Y	Newport
PKG739R	Shamrock	RBO506Y	Cardiff Bus	RKG427Y	Cardiff Bus	RUJ350R	Watts
PKG741R	Red & White	RBO507Y	Cardiff Bus	RMB403V	Express	RWN727Y	Merlyn's
PNH182	Shamrock	RBO508Y	Cardiff Bus	ROD662N	Len Hopkins	SBA201R	East End
PNK1M	Thomas Coaches	RBO509Y	Cardiff Bus	ROK452M	Coastal Continental	SBR87P	Howells Coaches
PNK154R	Perry's Supreme	RBO510Y	Cardiff Bus	ROK459M	Coastal Continental	SDA509S	Thomas Coaches
PNW604W	Glyn Williams	RDT121X	Wilkins Travel	ROM125M	Porthcawl Omnibus	SDA532S	Thomas Coaches
PNY391R	Porthcawl Omnibus	REA946W	Ken Hopkins	ROU348S	Wilkins Travel	SDA631S	Thomas Coaches
PPC335W	Wheadon's G'hound	REG480R	Wilkins Travel	RPE457R	Llynfi Coaches	SDA659S	Thomas Coaches
PPH432R	Edwards Coaches	RGE900W	John's Travel	RPR715R	East End	SDD141R	Edwards Coaches
PPH473R	Burrows	RHB305R	Shamrock	RPR751K	Mansell David	SDZ6287	Capitol Coaches
PRS517R	Hawthorn	RHG314K	East End	RPV673R	Llynfi Coaches	SEL128R	Hawthorn
PSD521R	Wilkins Travel	RHM928Y	C & E Travel	RRP861R	East End	SFD254W	Merlyn's
PSN916Y	Morris Travel	RIW4963	Diamond Glantawe	RSG814V	Red & White	SHE533Y	Jones of Bryncethin
PTG93Y	Newport	RIW4964	Diamond Glantawe	RSG815V	Red & White	SHP693R	Llynfi Coaches
PTG95Y	Newport	RJI2724	Nelson's Travel	RSG818V	Glyn Williams	SIB6740	I B T
PTG96Y	Newport	RJI8029	Brewers	RSG821V	Glyn Williams	SIB7240	Pullman Coaches
PTG97Y	Newport	RJI8030	Brewers	RSG823V	Red & White	SIJ408	Cyril Evans
PTG98Y	Newport	RJI8031	Brewers	RSG824V	Red & White	SIW2763	Diamond Glantawe

Reg	Operator	Reg	Operator	Reg	Operator	Reg	Operator
SJI2449	Edwards Coaches	UKE827X	Diamond Glantawe	WKG287	Henley's	XCY372T	Brian Issac
SKG895S	Mansell David	ULJ252J	Edwards Coaches	WMU43T	Thomas Coaches	XDG57S	Watts
SKG906S	Shamrock	ULJ253J	Edwards Coaches	WNO484	S W T	XDL794L	Shamrock
SKG908S	Red & White	ULJ257J	T R C	WOI3003	Brian Issac	XFM203	Newport
SKG923S	Red & White	ULJ260J	Edwards Coaches	WOI3004	Brian Issac	XHK234X	Brewers
SLO513R	Hawkes	ULJ264J	Edwards Coaches	WPD29Y	Morris Travel	XHR104	Edwards Coaches
SMY634X	Porthcawl Omnibus	ULS621X	Cardiff Bluebird	WSU472	Ken Hopkins	XJA515L	Edwards Coaches
SND293X	Edwards Coaches	ULS668T	Hawkes	WSV469	Rees Travel	XJF156S	T R C
SND295X	Edwards Coaches	UNW10M	Hawkes	WSV556	Rees Travel	XLB821	Mansell David
SND303X	Wilkins Travel	URN160R	Thomas Coaches	WTG328T	Venture Travel	XRD23K	East End
SOI196	Edwards Coaches	URN161R	Waterhall	WTG334T	Venture Travel	XRU281K	Edwards Coaches
STD179L	Edwards Coaches	URN162R	Waterhall	WTG335T	Cardiff Bus	XRW511S	Jones of Bryncethin
STJ847L	East End	URN163R	Thomas Coaches	WTG336T	Cardiff Bus	XSV695	Ferris Holidays
STJ850L	East End	URN164R	Thomas Coaches	WTG338T	Cardiff Bus	XVJ771	White Lion
SUH859M	Castell Coaches	UTV220S	T R C	WTG339T	Cardiff Bus	XVV540S	Red & White
SVO782R	Wilkins Travel	UTX726S	Red & White	WTG340T	Cardiff Bus	XWG652T	Cardiff Bluebird
SWP888V	Shamrock	UUP460R	Len Hopkins	WTG341T	Cardiff Bus	XWS541V	Martin
TDL483X	Welsh Dragon	UWO240S	Henley's	WTG342T	Cardiff Bus	XWU339S	Welsh Dragon
TDL566K	Hawkes	UWW518X	Cardiff Bluebird	WTG344T	Cardiff Bus	XWX172S	Shamrock
TDT1L	Thomas Coaches	UWW519X	Cardiff Bluebird	WTG345T	Cardiff Bus	XXI7360	Ken Hopkins
TDW312J	Phillips	VAY310S	Hawkes	WTG346T	Cardiff Bus	YAP104	Edwards Coaches
TDW315J	Edwards Coaches	VBA176S	Phillips	WTG347T	Cardiff Bus	YAW844T	Edwards Coaches
TDW318J	Edwards Coaches	VBG83V	Glyn Williams	WTG348T	Cardiff Bus	YBO150T	Rhondda
THH287X	Hawthorn	VBM716W	Wilkins Travel	WTG349T	Cardiff Bus	YBX469M	Diamond Glantawe
THL296Y	Watts	VBM948W	Martin	WTG350T	Cardiff Bus	YDD133S	Martin
THX145S	Hawkes	VCL461	Brewers	WTG351T	Cardiff Bus	YDW400T	Rhondda
THX161S	Harris	VEG155S	Rhondda	WTG353T	Cardiff Bus	YDW401T	Glyn Williams
THX191S	Shamrock	VFH700S	Diamond Glantawe	WTG354T	Cardiff Bus	YDW565T	I B T
THX213S	Shamrock	VHB673S	Shamrock	WTG355T	Cardiff Bus	YDW566T	I B T
THX218S	Shamrock	VJU125X	Phillips	WTG356T	Cardiff Bus	YDW758K	Newport
THX273S	Venture Travel	VKN835X	Porthcawl Omnibus	WTG359T	Cardiff Bus	YEV311S	S W T
TIB1224	Shamrock	VKN837X	Porthcawl Omnibus	WTG360T	Cardiff Bus	YEV315S	S W T
TIB5909	Burrows	VNB157L	Edwards Coaches	WTG361T	Cardiff Bus	YEV322S	S W T
TIB5912	Burrows	VNB173L	Edwards Coaches	WTG362T	Cardiff Bus	YFB5V	Jones of Bryncethin
TJI1698	Hawkes	VNH156W	East End	WTG365T	Cardiff Bus	YFB6V	Jones of Bryncethin
TJI1702	Pullman Coaches	VNT3S	Ken Hopkins	WTG366T	Cardiff Bus	YFB8V	Hawthorn
TJI4030	Pullman Coaches	VNT49S	Hawkes	WTG367T	Cardiff Bus	YFR494R	Hawthorn
TJI4123	Phil Anslow Travel	VOO235	Jones of Bryncethin	WTG368T	Cardiff Bus	YHY586J	Phil Anslow Travel
TJI4124	Phil Anslow Travel	VOR579T	Hawthorn	WTG369T	Cardiff Bus	YHY596J	Phil Anslow Travel
TJI4700	Pullman Coaches	VOY180X	Venture Travel	WTG370T	Cardiff Bus	YIA972	I B T
TJI5404	Merlyn's	VOY181X	Venture Travel	WTG373T	Cardiff Bus	YKG53	Edwards Coaches
TJI5405	Merlyn's	VPR489S	East End	WTG374T	Cardiff Bus	YLP528	Rhondda
TJI6320	Diamond Glantawe	VPR863S	Hawthorn	WTG375T	Cardiff Bus	YNA272M	Thomas Coaches
TND110X	Arthur Thomas	VVA7T	Waterhall	WTG376T	Cardiff Bus	YNA299M	Thomas Coaches
TRC883G	T R C	VVD433S	Hawthorn	WTG377T	Cardiff Bus	YNA369M	Thomas Coaches
TRT95M	Edwards Coaches	WAO644Y	Diamond Glantawe	WTG380T	Cardiff Bus	YNY58	Wheadon's G'hound
TWC298	White Lion	WAS767V	Red & White	WTG381T	Cardiff Bus	YNY588T	Hawkes
TWN801S	Brewers	WAX194S	Red & White	WTH171M	Porthcawl Omnibus	YPB840T	C & E Travel
TWN802S	S W T	WAX194S	Red & White	WTH959T	Brewers	YPC559Y	Watts
TWN803S	Brewers	WBN981L	Edwards Coaches	WTN647H	Edwards Coaches	YSU985	Thomas Coaches
TWS909T	Red & White	WCY701	Brewers	WUH166T	Red & White	YSV720	Brian Issac
TXI2425	Morris Travel	WDA1T	Red & White	WUH167T	Red & White	YSX926W	Red & White
TXI8759	White Lion	WDA2T	Red & White	WUH168T	Red & White	YSX927W	Glyn Williams
UAR587W	Brewers	WDA5T	Red & White	WUH174T	Glyn Williams	YSX932W	Red & White
UAR588W	Brewers	WEB409T	Mansell David	WWD106X	Phillips	YSX933W	Red & White
UAR598W	Brewers	WFX481	Nelson's Travel	WWN804T	S W T	YSX934W	Red & White
UCY843S	Porthcawl Omnibus	WGB298W	Burrows	WWN805T	S W T	YSX935W	Red & White
UDG206R	Venture Travel	WGT1	Thomas Coaches	WWN806T	Brewers	YTE113H	Diamond Glantawe
UDW939S	I B T	WHN462M	East End	WWN809T	Brewers	YTE115H	Diamond Glantawe
UHW10T	G M	WHN463M	East End	WWO811T	Phillips	YVC20L	Perry's Supreme
UIB3987	Diamond Glantawe	WHN468M	East End	WXI5863	I B T	YWN721	Merlyn's
UIJ742	Cyril Evans	WJX478V	Merlyn's	WXI9255	Ken Hopkins	YYE273T	Harris
UJI1765	Nelson's Travel	WKE69S	G M	WYM675	Ken Hopkins	YYE282T	Shamrock
UKE416H	G M			XBO117T	Mansell David		

ISBN 1 897990 18 9
Published by *British Bus Publishing*
The Vyne, 16 St Margarets Drive, Wellington,
Telford, Shropshire, TF1 3PH

Printed by Graphics & Print
Unit A13, Stafford Park 15
Telford, Shropshire, TF3 3BB

The South Wales Bus Handbook